IT HAS TO HURT

IT HAS
TO HURT

ACCEPTING LIFE'S HARSH REALITY, FINDING YOURSELF

ALONG THE WAY, AND ACTUALLY ENJOYING THE JOURNEY

LUIS RAUL SCOTT JR.

LIONCREST
PUBLISHING

IT HAS TO HURT
Accepting Life's Harsh Reality, Finding Yourself along the Way, and Actually Enjoying the Journey

FIRST EDITION

ISBN   978-1-5445-4122-8   *Hardcover*
        978-1-5445-4121-1   *Paperback*
        978-1-5445-4120-4   *Ebook*

This book is dedicated to my sons, Ruly and Lincoln. That one day you grow to be men who overcome all adversities, fears, and doubts and lead your families better than I was ever able to do.

CONTENTS

INTRODUCTION

I cannot believe I'm here again.

How did I manage to lose another job? How on earth did I let my house go into foreclosure? Another car repossessed. Another failed relationship. Another botched opportunity.

How do I keep letting these things happen?

If any of these thoughts have ever crept into your mind and kept you up, night after night, you are not alone. If you've ever thought, "There has to be more to life than this," either in the back of your mind as you wander through life, or out loud as one roadblock after another seems to obstruct your path, you are just one of the countless people in this world who are yearning for a more fulfilling life. Maybe you constantly wonder when your breakthrough is going to happen. When are you going to get that promotion? When are you going to get the pay raise you deserve? Maybe you feel like you're on the treadmill of life, finding it difficult to sustain meaningful relationships or discover your own potential, possibly even letting an embarrassing moment paralyze you from taking the next step.

I know you're not alone, because I have been there. That was me for eighteen years. I let myself play the victim, convinced life was happening to me and there was nothing I could do about it. I hung around in negativity and continued to believe "the best just wasn't for me." I ignored my true purpose, opting instead to live a life others expected of me. I let fear of judgment, ridicule, and criticism keep me from realizing my own greatness as I wondered over and over again, *When am I going to stop getting the short end of the stick?*

I let my circumstances determine my happiness instead of finding happiness in my circumstances. It was a drug for me, and I was an addict. An addict to pain. An addict to turmoil. An addict to feeling down. An addict to feeling defeated. An addict to misery.

The worst part was no one knew my struggle and my hardship. To some extent I didn't even know what was happening to me. On the outside I looked happy and normal, but on the inside, I was completely empty.

I searched and searched for the solution. I thought if I just had more money that would solve everything. I thought if I had a different marriage that would solve everything. Maybe if I had a better business that would solve everything. I traded everything out for the new, thinking that would take the feelings of inadequacy away.

Nothing worked. I was still empty.

Then something finally clicked in my life. Something that radically changed me forever.

I finally made the connection that happiness is not up to anyone or anything else. It was up to me owning and understanding my own identity. It was up to me seeing past fear and rising above negativity. It was up to me finding my passion, embracing failure, and letting go of control. But doing all of those things was not going to be easy.

Flash forward and today, I'm the COO of a $35 million law

firm with more than 150 employees. I am the founder of a consulting business that manages law firms around the country with revenues of close to $200 million. The past fifteen years were filled with hard work, unimaginable hardship, and gut-wrenching soul searching as I tapped into the person I was meant to be. Now, using all the lessons I learned along the way, I want to help you avoid the same mistakes, clear a path toward finding your true self, and enjoy a life of personal fulfillment and success you may never even think is possible.

GETTING OFF THE TREADMILL

For far too long, I let the idea that life was trying to hold me back keep me from moving forward toward the life I really wanted. I felt like I was always getting shortchanged (maybe you can relate?). I became familiar with the feeling early in life. My dad was in the military, and my family moved several times during my childhood. I spent most of my formative years in Puerto Rico, but by my high school years we were living in Georgia. I had been playing my favorite sport of all time, baseball, for years by then, and I made the school team as a freshman. However, I soon found out the coach's son played the exact same position I did. He was a year older than me, and you can guess what that meant for my playing time. Just imagine how that affected a kid who, like every other kid on the team, had his sights set on playing professional ball. It was the first time I remember feeling as if everything was working against me. A simple coincidence was keeping me from doing what I wanted, and I felt like I had no control over it. At the time it didn't matter if I was better or he was better—in my mind, I was a victim of something I could not control. Why couldn't he have been three years older than me? Why couldn't I have been older than him? At thirteen, everything seems amplified in life. I did not have the ability to process what was happening correctly.

In the background I could hear my dad telling me to relax. He would tell me, "God was in control." But man, if God was in control, what kind of crazy game was he playing?

While this scenario happened in my early teens, my reaction to it became something I carried with me and applied to every situation when things weren't working out the way I wanted them to. I played the victim when it came to everything, from not getting the job I wanted to being stuck with roommates I didn't want to live with to being in a relationship that wasn't as fulfilling as I wanted it to be. In my mind, nothing was my doing and I wasn't willing to take any responsibility for any of it. I did not have the personal or professional maturity to understand these events in context.

But the problems persisted as I got older. I continued to struggle with this sense of feeling that the world was crashing down on me.

If this wasn't bad enough, I also started struggling with a sense of life passing me by. At twenty years old, I already felt like I was running out of time. I wanted to rush life. I couldn't understand why my big breakthrough was not happening yet. Thank God there was not social media when I was going through this. I can't even imagine how much more difficult it would have been to go through all that while being able to scroll through the highlights of others' lives with the tap of a finger. I felt defeated enough at the time.

I have always felt intense pressure to do everything I wanted *right this minute*. Never mind all the evidence showing how many people become successful later in their life. Colonel Sanders was in his sixties when he founded KFC. Vera Wang didn't make her first dress until she was forty. That never mattered to me—to me, success needed to come as soon as possible or I was doing something very wrong. I was desperate. Desperate for acceptance. Desperate for achievement. Desperate for validation. I wanted my life to mean something and there was no time to waste.

Today, we tend to treat this as a problem unique to the millennial generation. But this is an everybody problem. When we are unfulfilled in life, every moment can feel like a minute too long.

I felt like I was stuck on the treadmill of life. I remember feeling as if no matter what I did, I could never get ahead. I couldn't make more money. I couldn't get the job I wanted. I couldn't get a business off the ground. In my mind, I had to get everything done so quickly that when I wasn't successful in year one, two, or three, those became wasted years. It wasn't until I was thirty-five years old that I realized all those years actually were building blocks creating the foundation of who I am today. When I coach people in their twenties, I tell them it took me thirty-five years to figure it out and five more years to become an overnight success. But those years were tough.

WHEN WE ARE UNFULFILLED IN LIFE, EVERY MOMENT CAN FEEL LIKE A MINUTE TOO LONG.

MAKING THE CONNECTION

It's taken me years to realize the reason most of us don't get the breakthrough we want is because *we're simply not ready for it*. We haven't lived enough, experienced enough, grown enough to know how to handle getting and keeping the thing we really want in this life. We like to talk the talk, but when it comes to walking the walk, many of us have no idea how to even start because we're focusing on the wrong goals.

Many people, unfortunately, have high ambition but low endurance and work ethic. Because most people are not willing to work long enough or hard enough for their goals and dreams, they oftentimes live in complete misery. For example, I have had the ambition of developing six-pack abs for years, but my endurance in the gym and the kitchen has not matched that ambition. I oftentimes spend the day either being upset about not reaching my goal or making excuses as to why it's too hard for me to attain. The fact of the matter is that neither complaining about it nor excusing it actually helps me achieve it.

By tapping into your full potential and becoming the person you need to be, you instantly add more value to your life. When you add more value, you're going to get paid more. When you get paid more, you're going to have money to save, and when you save, you're going to have that house or any other thing you set your sights on. But here's the catch about using your life experiences to help you tap into your true identity: it has to hurt. Because life hurts. Relationships hurt. Failures hurt. Disappointments hurt. Falling down hurts. Let's face it, most things in life hurt. And if you want to stand tall, you will experience pain in your life.

In the past several years I have felt many of these pains. The road to success has been paved by the pains of everyday life experiences. It has been in those experiences that I have developed into the person I was created to be. However, when I was going through it all, much of it felt like agony.

I never would have become the person I am today without the building blocks of the last fifteen years and all of the hardships and challenges that came with them. The experience has taught me that you can choose to let negativity drag you down, or you can rise above it and realize this life is a journey. That journey will have many low points along the way, but if you learn how to trust the process, you will take those challenges and turn them into opportunities for growth and prosperity.

This might sound too easy if you've gone through or are currently experiencing a particularly dark period of your life. Believe me—it's not. I've experienced many low points of my own, and I can tell you every challenge in my life taught me a lesson about how to take all the negativity, all the setbacks, all the hurdles and use them to become the person I was truly meant to be in this world.

MY DEPRESSION

To compound the agony I suffered in life, I realized at almost thirty-eight years old that I suffered from depression. Living in what has felt like a cruel world left me jaded, which made it particularly difficult for me to cope with hardship. I held on to the pain. I held on to the hurt. I held on to the disappointment. I held on to the suffering. I replayed every negative situation in my mind over and over and over again until it felt real almost every moment of my adult life.

From crying on the shower floor to driving in complete silence for hours on end, I endured the last twenty years of my life in utter mental anguish.

And to make it worse, I did it all alone in silence without anyone knowing. Not only did I not really understand my depression, but I never let anyone know about it either. I bottled it all inside for the fear of appearing weak. Even as my entire life was crashing down, I believed I could fix it all on my own.

I tried to "fix" my depression by reading books. I think I read *The Power of Positive Thinking* twenty times. But nothing worked. As a religious person I spent hours praying. I did a seven-day, ten-day, and twenty-one-day fast. I went to the gym. I picked up playing the piano. But nothing would ease the pain of my past hurts. Every pain and hurt would compound on the next, and my soul felt the heaviness. My ex-wife used to tell me she thought I was a tortured soul, but she didn't know how to reach out to me.

It was a grueling twenty years. Fortunately, by the grace of God, I overcame it. Not by some method, but rather by a commitment. I made a commitment before I even knew I was battling with depression that I would never give up hope for a better future. I was never going to give up. NEVER!

When I finally found out I was battling depression all of these years, I continued to reaffirm the commitment to myself of never giving up. I would reaffirm that I didn't have to live the next thirty or forty more years in pain. I only needed to finish living today. And every day that was my decision: to live today.

This is the first time I have ever opened up publicly about the depression I have faced all of these years. I'm talking about it here so you understand the stories I tell in this book are through the eyes of a person who didn't fully understand the condition from which he suffered. This is not a book about overcoming or managing depression—it is a book about developing the skills you need to overcome any hardship in your life to get to the place you want to be. Just understand that everything I was experiencing at the time was essentially distorted through the lens of depression in my mind. The facts are true. The assumptions I made, however, may not have been. The lessons I learned along the way are the new truth by which I live my life.

A BETTER LIFE AWAITS

In these pages, you're going to learn about the pain I went through and how I used that pain to create a new self and a true identity. You'll learn how such a drastic change did not happen overnight but took years and years of looking critically at my life, my choices, and what version of myself I was giving to the world. As Rachel Hollis wrote in *Girl, Wash Your Face,* "Nothing that lasts is accomplished quickly. Nobody's entire legacy is based on a single moment but rather the collection of one's experiences. If you're lucky, your legacy will be a lifetime in the making."

What I've learned over my life is that finding real, lasting success is not like becoming a one-hit wonder. There will not be one moment or one accomplishment that will lead you to lasting, sustainable prosperity. Think of every one-hit wonder you know: you likely can hum the tune, but do you know what happened to that singer after their hit faded from the charts? No one does, and that's not the kind of life you want to have. If you're reading this book, it's because you want a life that leaves a lasting impact for years, decades, maybe even generations to come.

But right now, you might feel as if life's challenges are determining your course. Perhaps you've had a business failure or financial hardship. Maybe lingering self-doubt is keeping you rooted where you are. You're likely not happy in your job yet letting it dictate just about every decision in your life. Maybe you are like me, dealing with all of the above and also battling depression.

And yet, despite all this, you might also feel as if you're somehow destined for greatness. Do you have a sense there is actually something better out there for you, something greater about you, something special you can share with the world?

Something only you can provide to this world before you die, and without you the world will be worse off?

If that's how you feel, good—because the truth is, no matter where you are in your life right now, you are meant to be the A-lister of your story. You are not the supporting cast or the crew. Your life is the show, and you are the star.

In this book I want to provide you hope. That hope will come through an understanding that your circumstances do not need to define your life. That your disappointments do not need to define your life. That your hardships do not need to define your life. That depression does not need to define your life. That everything you go through can be the catalyst for a new life and a new day. That you have meaning and that your life has meaning no matter the circumstances and no matter how difficult life may become.

This book is going to show you how to take all the hardships you've experienced and turn them into positives. It will prove that everyone goes through hardships—in fact, without them, you *can't* become successful. No one can become who they were intended to be without the hardships that refine and sharpen us. Iron sharpens iron. It takes the clinging together of two sharp objects to really make you sharp, and sometimes those sharp objects will cut you. They can hurt you, but without taking the risk of refining yourself and polishing who you are as a person, you're never going to be who you were intended to be and you're always going to feel stuck.

All of my experiences overcoming life's challenges have taught me that in reality, no one is truly stuck. No one is alone, and even though bad things happen, everybody can get through them and so can you. It won't always be easy—in fact, it rarely will be. You'll want to avoid the hard things. You'll want to go under them, over them, beside them, and around them. But the only way to become who you were created to be is to go *through* them, allowing the journey to make you stronger. To reap the real benefits of the experience, you have to be willing to take on the responsibility of being disciplined and of having endurance for the thing you know in your heart you were created for.

Maybe you want to lose weight. That means you're going to have to be willing to get up in the morning, every single morning, and go to the gym or go run *even when you don't want to*. Maybe you want to grow in your profession. You're going to have to be willing to get up early in the morning or stay up late and read and learn and become a master at what you do. Maybe you want to get out of debt. You're going to have to be willing to sacrifice the vacation, the nice car, the nice shoes, the daily latte, whatever it takes to make that happen for yourself.

No matter your goal, there is going to be something in your life that's going to try to hold you back. The question is: are you willing to move through those things so you can truly access the life you were created to live? If your answer is yes, the very first thing you have to do is figure out who you really are and how you can best use your unique strengths to start being the person you were put on this earth to be. (If your answer is no, you should probably put this book down now.) If you want to avoid pain and hurt, you are destined to experience a lot of disappointment. Only when we are intentional in accepting that pain is unavoidable in life do we begin to rid ourselves of the self-imposed restrictions we have placed on our lives. We begin to live when we realize that pain is just part of living. We begin to feel when we realize hurt feelings are simply part of the journey.

This book will teach you to start by speaking truthfully about yourself and the things you want and embracing the rent life requires you to pay. As it says in the Bible, "Out of the abundance of the heart, the mouth will speak." What's in your heart is what you will say, and what you say is what you will live. You become the destiny you speak because at the end of the day, whatever you're speaking, you're hearing. The more you say something, the more you will believe it. If you say you're not capable, you will render yourself incapable. If you say you can't lose weight, you will never lose weight. If you say you'll never get a promotion, get comfortable in the job you're in because you're staying there. You have to learn to stop talking yourself out of achieving your goals, but to do so takes understanding who you are at your core and why that person is deserving of everything they want. You have to stop believing everyone is against you and start believing in you. Once you get your mind, body, and spirit right, you will stop believing the lies you have chosen to let rule you, and you will be on a path to a greater life.

WHO AM I?

It's a question I'm going to ask you to seriously consider later on, but for now, let me answer by telling you a little about my own life's journey. I was born in Gary, Indiana, the son of two Puerto Rico natives who came to the States so my dad could work in the local church. We lived there for several years then moved to Puerto Rico and bounced back and forth between there and the States depending on where my dad was stationed for the first thirteen years of my life. Basically, my entire childhood was one big culture shock.

I ate Puerto Rican food. I celebrated the holidays celebrated in Puerto Rico. I was surrounded by a Puerto Rican family. We spoke Spanish all the time. Yet, I also had an Americanized identity. Growing up, it was hard to know who I really was. When people asked me where I was from, I never knew what to say. Was I from Indiana? Puerto Rico? The former didn't seem right because I'd only lived there a few years. The latter could be misleading as I didn't feel fully connected to Puerto Rican culture because I left there when I was thirteen. There were a lot of factors keeping me from really understanding my true identity, and at times, it made me question who I was.

Add to all this confusion the fact that I'm a dark-skinned Puerto Rican with light-skinned siblings. In Puerto Rico, that never mattered. There, you have people who are light-skinned, dark-skinned, middle of the road, blonds, redheads, green eyes, blue eyes, all of it. In the States, you have African Americans, White Americans, Asian Americans, Native Americans. In Puerto Rico, nobody is Afro Puerto Rican or Anglo Puerto Rican—everybody's just Puerto Rican. There's no distinction between the color or background. At least that had been my experience. There's a huge mixture, but everybody considers themselves to be Puerto Rican. In the States, skin color was a frequent issue. I always felt people were judging me because of my skin, and I was the victim of racism on several occasions which, over time, began to chip away at my sense of identity.

Another thing not helping matters was my name: Luis Raul Scott Jr. People couldn't understand how I had a Puerto Rican background but Scott as a last name, which sounds very Americanized. The background is complicated: there's a history of slavery on my father's side and rather than take on the name of the lineage, which should have been Morales, everybody kept the slave name, which was Scott. My dad didn't even know this until later in life, and he opted to stay Scott.

Even the pronunciation of my name was complicated. Growing up I was known as Raullin by my family. In elementary school I was called Luisito. In high school, everyone called me Lou-is (like Lewis), so that's what I answered to. My lack of self-worth and inability to see my own value kept me from ever correcting anyone. I let it go on for years until finally I got to college, and people started to call me Loo-ees (the correct Spanish pronunciation of my name), and everyone else picked up on it. From that point on, I decided to own my name and not make excuses about it, which helped (for the record, people call me just about anything today—Lewis, Luis, Lu. I'm fine with all of it). But I always introduce myself with the Spanish pronunciation of Luis.

That was a hard time. I was culturally Hispanic, but many people thought I was black. I didn't fit in with the "true Hispanics" and I didn't fit in with the whites. And I didn't fit in with the blacks. I felt isolated. It took a long time for me to move past those feelings and stop letting how others saw me define who I was and shape my sense of self. When I was twenty-one years old, I had to write a short bio of myself for a public speaking class. I remember thinking about it, then writing, "Luis is from Naguabo, Puerto Rico." It finally just felt good. I began to own my heritage, and it became my story from that point on. I began to learn as much as I could about Puerto Rico. I read about its history. I learned where I was from. Now, any time somebody asks me where I'm from, I always say Puerto Rico. I owned that identity regardless of whether people thought I deserved it or not.

My identity was further complicated because of the depression. I rejected all things that did not make me happy. I was angry at who I had become, not knowing I was being transformed into something I never wanted to be. As a victim I blamed everyone for my lack of happiness and contentment. I didn't know if I was coming or going. All I knew was that where I was currently was not where I wanted to be.

You'll learn much more about my journey in the coming

chapters. For now, I'll tell you that today, I co-own one of the largest law firms in the state of Georgia. My business partner and I employ more than 150 people. We co-own a successful seven-figure consulting company, and we also have a property holding company. It didn't come quickly or easily, but I am now the person I was always meant to be: a successful entrepreneur and married father of three living a full and happy life. I still battle with the depression, but now I don't use my bad days to reject all of the good days. I recognize that my pain has been the catalyst for becoming who God created me to be, and that is something I could never have become without the things I endured.

But it all started with me figuring out who I really was.

OPERATING IN YOUR TRUE LIGHT

This book is a personal journey story. It's the story of a man who grew up in different cultures and who experienced a tremendous amount of failure in his life both personally and professionally. But it's also a story of how that same person found redemption through never wavering in the belief he was made for something more.

This book is the story of someone who lost his way because of decisions he made, but who was able, through a great deal of reflection and character building, to find the path to success. It's about a man who started out accepting victimhood, staying in failed relationships, allowing criticism and naysayers to control his life, but who then chose to rebuild by becoming the person he was created to be. This is a book about a depressed man who works daily to conquer his burden in life to become someone his kids are proud of.

This book is not a quick fix. It's not going to take away all your problems or pain. It will, however, challenge you to confront those issues and work through them to strengthen your sense of self and point you in the direction you are meant to travel because ultimately…it has to hurt. Life is full of hardship. People will die. People will leave, abandon, and betray you. The question is: are you willing to stand firm in knowing who you are so you can cope with the problems in your life? Are you willing to believe you were made for more? Are you willing to accept that you have something to contribute to this world no matter how hard it may get?

If so, this book will help you form a strategy to do just that. It will help you identify who you are so you can engage in your true passion and develop a legacy that will impact people for generations to come. Because when you operate in your true light, it radiates to other people.

It all starts with you and your willingness and ability to tap into the person you were meant to be. Let's get started.

CHAPTER ONE

IT'S ALL ABOUT YOU

WHY IDENTITY IS THE FOUNDATION OF EVERYTHING

"Too many of us are not living our dreams because we're living our fears."

—LES BROWN

When I was in my late twenties, I made one of the dumbest financial decisions I've ever made: I sunk $32,000 into a car. But not just any car. It was a used X5 BMW SUV, and I was *so proud* of it. I thought it was the coolest vehicle in the world. In my mind, that car meant I had arrived. My identity was rooted in embodying the image of the ultra-successful BMW owner, and I was loving every minute of it. Because the truth is the only reason I got the BMW was because I wanted to impress other people. I wanted everyone to be blown away by the fact that I had enough money to buy such a luxurious car. I wanted them to see me driving in it and make the natural assumption that I was large and in charge. I wanted the car to elevate my status in the minds of others, and I wanted all the admiration that went along with that. (I've now realized that car was not that luxurious at all and there are people I know paying upwards of $300,000 for cars.)

Turned out, the car was a lemon. It nickel-and-dimed me to the tune of $10,000 in the first year of ownership, and after all that frustration, I ended up selling it for $10,000 less than what it was worth. The BMW, which I had for one year, cost me $12,000 in payments, $10,000 to "fix," and another $10,000 in depreciated value to sell. I sunk $32,000 into owning a vehicle in one year. That $32,000, which was supposed to help me impress people, ended up having the exact opposite effect. Most people couldn't believe I had bought such a crappy car. They asked, "What were you thinking? Did you not test drive it? Why on earth did you do this to yourself?"

The answer was simple: I cared more about what other people thought about me than what I thought about myself. Other people's opinions mattered so much because my entire self-worth depended on the words of my peers. It wasn't pride, although that's what most people called it. It was actually the opposite of pride. I was feeling worthless, and I needed the words of others to build my worth. I needed the affirmation that I was good enough. I needed the affirmation that I was successful enough. I thought the car was my ticket. In the end it caused me incredible financial pain.

In my life, I have spent an inordinate amount of time worrying about how people see me. I can't tell you how many hours I've wasted wondering, *Does that person think I'm worthy? Do they think I'm capable? Does this girl/teacher/coach/pastor/family member approve of me?* In fact, I wasted so much time worrying about those things, I never stopped to consider what *I* thought about me, and because of that, I began to make decisions that were contrary to my own personal self-worth and sense of identity. I made decisions based on how I thought other people viewed me to try to meet their expectations, but I was not meeting my own. I was consumed with the unspoken thoughts of other people. And let me tell you, that is no way to live. It took me down a spiral staircase to nowhere.

All too often, many of us let the fear of failing to live up to other people's standards dictate the course of our own lives. We work tirelessly to make sure people find us valuable and "approve" of us instead of working on figuring out who we actually are as individuals. But what people say or think about you doesn't really matter at all. In truth, what really matters is *what you say about you.*

You are responsible for being your own greatest cheerleader, and to do that, you have to train yourself to say and think the right things about yourself in order to become the person you were created to be. Too many times, we let other people's words and thoughts make us victims when in reality, other people are facing their own giants.

MANY OF US LET THE FEAR OF FAILING TO LIVE UP TO OTHER PEOPLE'S STANDARDS DICTATE THE COURSE OF OUR OWN LIVES.

YOU CAN'T COMPARE

Most of us are obsessed with what people think because we have an innate tendency to measure ourselves against others. The comparison game is something you will never win. There will always be someone with a better car, better house, more attractive spouse, better-behaved kids, and more money. Comparing is a sure way to keep you in a depressed state of mind. I know because I have lived most of my life in that state.

We all have a competitive spirit within us that drives us to do better than the other people in our lives. The need to "keep up with the Joneses" is practically a national epidemic causing a lot of people a great deal of stress. With social media it has been blown to epic proportions as we spend most of our time comparing our everyday lives to the highlight reels of other people. Lines form outside of designer stores and people spend hours a day sharing all of the successes of their lives. We see life as a zero-sum game: if someone else is winning, it means we're losing and that's not acceptable. I see it all the time with employees who obsess over the latest trends in an attempt to impress others. They want the car only so others see them as successful. They want to have the social media–approved vacation. And temporarily, it works. We get what we want by impressing our peers. People say "cool car" or "nice house." But that eventually fades, and we end up chasing the next compliment. All the while, we never end up finding any true satisfaction or happiness. The treadmill of validation never ends, and the power source never depletes. No matter how big your house is or how cool your car is, it will never be enough to give you a lifetime of validation. So, the treadmill continues running.

This drive is primitive, likely the result of a time when resources were scarce and "losing" meant true suffering. Even if you watch small children today, when one gets something, the others instantly want it. It doesn't matter what it is—they just *want* it. Nobody has to teach them to want it. Their brains are making comparisons before they even fully understand the concept: "He got three presents, and I only got two. I can't stand for that." Even when the two presents are worth more than the three, what matters is not reality but perception.

Finding real, sustainable happiness requires fighting that natural inclination. You must learn to stop comparing yourself to anyone else and understand the only person you have to be better than is the person you were yesterday. You only need to be satisfied with you.

Comparing who you are today to your former self can take work. My dad tells me life is like a golf game. You're not measuring your performance against other people's games—you're measuring it against your own. Is your game improving every single time you play? In other words, are you using each day as an opportunity to better who you are and how you see yourself? My dad's constant reminder to me has always been, "Golf is better when you keep your own score."

The only way to do so is to focus on your own score. If the course is par 72 but I compete with a guy who shoots an 85, my win with an 82 isn't great. Sure, I'd be better than him, but I'd still not be a very good player. Instead of improving my game for the sake of improving my game, I'd only improve enough to beat him and therefore, hold myself to a standard lower than what I might be capable of. We do the same thing in many areas of our lives. We don't say, "How can I get better at being a lawyer so I can be the best lawyer I can be?" We say, "How can I be a better lawyer than the guy I work with? How can I be a better lawyer than the guy that I'm going to be going against?" We ask, "How can I make more money than the lawyers I know?" as if that is the determining factor of success in our lives. I know attorneys who earn more than me but have a much smaller impact. Comparing ourselves to the next person is a recipe for stress, not success.

SOCIAL IMPACT

Quashing our desire to constantly compare ourselves to others is particularly tricky in the day of social media. These tools are great when used correctly and can help you build your business and brand—but this is true only if you know who you are, and many people don't. They have yet to discover their true passion; they have no idea what they were created for. For these people, social media can do far more harm than good. Social media is a highlight reel, and all too often, people compare their everyday lives to the highlights of all of their friends. You will never win that game because the highlights are just too good.

For people who haven't achieved the level of success they seek, social media is the only access they have to a life they otherwise don't think they can live. They see people going to upscale restaurants every day, traveling to fun places every weekend, and seemingly living life to the fullest. Meanwhile, because they have no idea who they are or what their true purpose is, they go to their unfulfilling jobs day after day, sit in their crappy apartments, eat the same boring food, and do nothing exciting. Now, their lack of self-worth is multiplied. Whereas before they knew other people were doing things but didn't have the proof shoved under their noses every hour, they now can scroll Facebook and see everybody's highlight reel. Everybody's posting about the great gym workout they just did. Everybody's posting their vacation photos. Summer is the worst, when it's nothing but beach pictures. It's as if everyone is going to the most exotic spots all over the world. What they don't tell you is they probably saved for two years to go on that one-week vacation. Or maybe they put it on the credit card and live in terrible debt. All you see is that beautiful scenery and their smiling faces.

Social media prevents us from developing our own identity because now we view ourselves through the lens of someone else's fake life. It's important to remember the carefully curated images of one person's life are never indicative of the whole picture. I know plenty of "happy" couples on social media that are on the brink of divorce.

THE DANGER OF NOT KNOWING YOURSELF

When you don't know who you are, it's easy to get caught up in the identity of someone else and compare yourself to other people constantly. For my teenage self, that someone was Justin Timberlake.

To remind you, I am a dark-skinned Puerto Rican. My hair is naturally curly, but if I blow it dry, it lies straight. In high school, I grew out my hair down to my forehead and cut it straight across. That's right—I gave myself bangs. Again, *nothing* about my physical appearance suggests I should have bangs. And yet, I did. I wanted to have the look Timberlake had in NSYNC. (And before you ask, no, I did not dye my hair bright blond. Maybe I should have. I can't imagine this look could have been worse, so why not?)

I had absolutely no idea who I was. I was struggling with my identity, particularly as it related my culture, given that I was both Puerto Rican and living in the country town of Harlem, Georgia. A lot of my friends were white, and I was singing with a few in a boy band because if you were a teen in the mid- to late-'90s, that was just what you did. The name was Chords of Soul. Everything about me was ridiculous (and yes, I did eventually realize that and grew out the bangs, only to grow a set of thick sideburns, but that's another story).

My tragic choice of hairstyle, while comical, is just one example of what can happen when you have absolutely no idea who you really are. The true danger of not knowing yourself is how easily you can be swayed to become something else entirely. You can become somebody you're not and end up with friends who are not at all in line with your core beliefs. In turn, you won't know your true value. And when you don't know your value, you take on the value other people put on you, and that's a real problem. You will never be satisfied with the value others place on you because people are flawed. Therefore, the value they have for you is flawed, even if well intentioned.

Furthermore, when you don't know who you are, you have no way of defending yourself when other people make unfair assumptions about you, as I experienced several times throughout my life.

CULTURE SHOCK

My first real experience with racism happened in my late teens. I was pumping gas into my little white two-door, nine-year-old BMW at a gas station in Savannah, Georgia. The car was a gift from my parents because between my athletic and academic scholarships, I had earned a full ride to college. I had rolled down my windows and was enjoying the salsa music playing on the radio. It was around 9:00 p.m. The music was not super loud—definitely no louder than the Harley motorcycle that had been blaring its muffler next to me.

The next thing I knew, police lights engulfed both me and my car and an officer pulled over right next to me. At this point in my life, I'd been in the United States for five years—long enough to know there were clear differences between whites and blacks but never experiencing a situation in which I felt like the direct victim of blatant racism. I am not one to pull the race card, but this stop was not normal.

The cop, in his most patronizing tone, said, "Boy, can you not read?" I was more confused than upset. "Yes, sir," I said, then, "Am I doing something wrong?" He asked, "You don't see that sign right there?" I looked where he pointed. There hung a sign advertising a city ordinance for noise control. It said anyone in violation would be subject to a $100 fine.

"I can hear your music across the street," the cop sneered as I read.

Granted, the music was loud enough for me to hear through my open window as I pumped gas. I highly doubt, however, anyone a pump or two over would even have noticed it. But nevertheless, the stop was not the issue. The officer's tone and the way he addressed me was.

He gave me the ticket for violation of a noise ordinance and was on his way. Even though I may have been in the wrong, that officer did exactly what he intended to do: he completely belittled me. He left me feeling small, less than. It made me start questioning what it meant to be a minority. I didn't know what I could do about it—I just knew I didn't ever want to be treated this way again.

I didn't realize at the time, but that cop's racist character had *nothing to do with me.* He chose to project his own prejudices and slanted way of seeing the world onto me. And because I did not know who I was or feel confident enough in my own identity, I let him. I absorbed his negative worldview rather than looking within and realizing nothing he saw in me was real—the only thing that was real was me, my own character, and the choices I made for myself in my own life. It affected me so much that I spent a large part of my twenties trying to explain my race. Any time I met someone new, I always led off with "I'm Puerto Rican." I would avoid the sun so that I would not get darker. I did not want to be profiled or treated any way because I was not white. But my skin color was something I was never going to be able to avoid. That moment with the cop hurt for me. It was something that scarred me in a way I could not describe. It stayed in my consciousness for decades as I tried to fight the idea that I was not worthy simply because I was not white.

What this incident taught me is that whether it's related to race, gender, or anything to do with your physical appearance, people are going to make assumptions about your identity. And if you are not firmly rooted in knowing who you are, you're going to take offense to everything. Once I learned this, I began taking assumptions people made about my race in stride because there's no reason for me to take offense to their ignorance. My dark skin leads many people to assume I'm black. Because my ex-wife is a very light-skinned Puerto Rican and our kids appear to be of mixed race, perfect strangers have no problem asking me, "Are your kids mixed?" I always respond, "Yes, they're a mix of me and their mom." Typically, the person who asked the question blusters, "No, no, no. That's not what I mean. Where are *you* from?" When I tell them I'm Puerto Rican, the next line is predictably, "Oh, so their mom is white." At this point, I usually say something along the lines of, "No, their mom is Puerto Rican." It never ceases to amaze me why those details matter so much to others, but by now, it has no effect on me or how I live my life. I just accept the fact that they are ignorant.

PERSONAL INJURY

I've also learned that when you don't know who you are, it's easy to let one aspect of your personality define you. But what happens when that one thing is taken away?

From a young age, my identity was wrapped up in the belief that I was going to become a professional baseball player. My dad saw the talent in me; I saw the talent in myself. He played Double A ball in Puerto Rico, and I felt I had the genes. I also had the work ethic and the dedication. But many times, our dreams do not materialize because of one thing or another. For me, it was a physical injury.

In high school the baseball coach was also the high school head football coach. In my senior year of high school, the football team found itself without a long snapper, so I stepped up. I don't know how I developed the talent for it—I simply could snap a ball really well. Plus, my coach said playing on the team would get me in good condition for baseball season. He knew I wanted to go pro, and he promised to never play me in another position where I'd be more likely to get injured. I had already played receiver and quarterback and I did not want to do anything to injure myself.

In October 1999, I snapped the ball to the kicker and took off running down the field. I was in position to tackle the opposing player. He went left. I went right. But suddenly, he pivoted and when I planted my foot to follow him, my whole knee gave out. I had torn my ACL.

In that moment, I thought my life was absolutely over. The dream I had held so close to my heart all my life was disappearing into thin air. I would not be playing baseball my senior year. The Cincinnati Reds scout who was coming to see me play that season would no longer consider me. With one plant of my foot, all my plans and hopes were ripped apart. I cried for three days.

I was so devastated at the idea of not playing baseball, I decided to forgo surgery, and I played my entire senior season with a torn ACL because at least that meant I could get out on the field. I simply could not even begin to think of who I was if I wasn't playing baseball. By some miracle, I had a great year and was team captain and defensive player of the year. The newspaper even did an article about me and the grit it took to play with my injury (I still have the clipping).

In my freshman year of college, I planned to red shirt, which is common for baseball players in their first year. I figured it would give me even more time to heal. But then the team's shortstop got injured, and they needed me to play. Now I didn't have a choice—I again had to play with a torn ACL.

Eleven days before my first game, I was going to grab a ball and my whole knee blew out—ACL, MCL, PCL, cartilage, everything. It was done. I could not even walk. They had to carry me off the field. Surgery was the only option, and even though I still had the drive and dedication to be a pro baseball player, I was starting to come to terms with the fact that it might never happen.

I was utterly defeated. It went beyond the physical—I felt injured in my heart, in my spirit, in my mind. It shocked me to realize I could no longer base my entire identity on my physical ability because twice in two years, it had been taken away from me, and I was unraveling. It forced me to look deep within myself and ask why I had let one aspect of my life yield so much power over me. I realized I'd allowed that to happen because I was running from my true purpose and desire, which it turned out was not to become a pro athlete. I felt like I was good at what I did, but I didn't feel like I was created to do it. I always had a nagging sense of doubt telling me, "This is not what I'm created to do, so therefore, I'm going to fail." My injuries were physical confirmation that I was going to continue to fail because this was not the path I was meant to travel.

I didn't know it at the time, but I was created to be a manager, the COO and owner of a big business. That, of course, would take time to manifest. Back then, I only knew the "dream" I'd carried for myself for so long was never meant to come to fruition, and it was tough to deal with.

Allowing one specific thing to define you is a trap many people fall into. They rest their entire identity on a job or a relationship or any other role they've assumed. But when they lose that job or that relationship, they lose all of who they are.

Learning the dangers of this helped me when I began facing hardship later in life. When my relationship with my first wife ended and again when I got fired from my partnership, I did not lose my sense of self because I knew I did not need to wrap my entire identity into one aspect of my life. No one's worth can be tied to one single thing. It doesn't make it easy, just easier than it otherwise would have been.

RISING ABOVE

Owning your identity and overcoming the judgment some people immediately place on you takes work. First, you simply have to accept what's out of your control. When it came to my skin color, there was nothing I could do. I am going to be a dark-skinned Puerto Rican for the entirety of my life. It's not limited to race— you're likely as tall as you're going to be or as short as you're going to be, you'll always have the eye color you have, the same bone structure, the same hair, because all of it is uniquely yours. You can try to manufacture something different to some degree (much like how I tried to manufacture myself into Justin Timberlake), but there are some things you just have to come to terms with.

Second, you have to realize the people who genuinely care about you and believe in you are far more important than those who want to drag you down. There are people who truly see you for who you are as a person and who will appreciate and value you for everything that makes you, you. Ten people who believe in you is more powerful than fifty who do not.

Third, understand that when it comes to owning your identity, you don't owe anyone an explanation for any part of you. For a long time, any time I met someone new, I felt as if I had to lay out my entire credentials for them: I'm Puerto Rican but I grew up in the States, I have a law degree, *blah, blah, blah.*

I finally realized I don't owe anyone that information. Now I understand that if I introduce myself to you and you don't like who I am, that's your problem, not mine. People who decide they don't like you will always find a reason to not like you. I've had four ex-employees call me fake, disingenuous, disrespectful, or rude, none of which are true of me but all of which other coworkers thought was true of those accusers. Projection at its finest. There's nothing you can do about it, and honestly, if they're the type of person who judges people based on their own insecurities and prejudices, why would you ever care?

OWNING WHO YOU ARE

Once you stop letting others define your identity, the real work begins. Now you have to confront who you truly are at your core, and for many people, that's terrifying. The process of self-discovery can be grueling. It's far easier to accept who other people say you are than to learn who you really are. Because once you know who you are, you have a responsibility to make yourself the best version of you you're capable of being. And it generally requires you walking into your destiny, which will always be met with criticism and opposition. I can't even count the number of people who have said they did not understand why I surpassed people who had been there longer than me to become partner of my law firm.

There is a passage in the Book of James in the Bible that basically says only a fool looks at their reflection in the mirror, walks away, and forgets who they are. The foolish person would rather forget because once they know who they are, they can't walk away and stay the same. They have to be different. Once you know you were made for more, you have a responsibility to become that person.

ONCE YOU STOP LETTING OTHERS DEFINE YOUR IDENTITY, THE REAL WORK BEGINS.

The process of finding who I am has taken me more than thirty years. I didn't realize I was great at business until I had already been doing it for about ten years. Actually, other people brought it to my attention. They'd say things like, "Man, I love talking to you about business. You have a really interesting perspective." Then the more I thought about how much I loved learning about business strategies and ways to become successful at it, the more I realized how passionate I was about it. I'm good at it because I am genuinely excited about it. But realizing that fact took years and much effort on my part to look within and realize why I was doing the work I was doing. Without the introspection, I would not have come to that conclusion.

The process of self-discovery is different for everyone. If your reflection brings you to the realization that you're on the wrong path, you have even more work to do. Most likely, correcting your path will require some degree of risk, especially if you've become complacent in the life you've created for yourself. Your enemy will be your own self-doubt. The fear of ridicule and self-consciousness we all experience, particularly as we begin to embark on a journey toward becoming the person we are meant to be, will threaten to hold you back. Fortunately, there are ways to confront these hurdles head-on and move past them with a stronger sense of self than you've ever previously had.

CHAPTER ONE EXERCISES

To begin to better understand your own identity, ask yourself:

- What three events in your life have shaped the way you think and feel about yourself in a good way?
- What three events in your life have shaped the way you think and feel about yourself in a bad way?
- In one paragraph, summarize who you believe you are today. Is it who you want to be? If not, what would need to happen for you to become the person you are supposed to be?
- Ask yourself: If I became who I was created to be, who would I become? Am I living that life?

CHAPTER TWO

STOP FEEDING YOUR FEARS

OVERCOMING WHAT'S REALLY HOLDING YOU BACK

"Everything you want is on the other side of fear."

—JACK CANFIELD

As you move through life, you might be convinced you are in charge of your decisions. You might think each move you make is driven solely by your sound conscious mind, completely devoid of any other influence. Unfortunately, you're wrong. The truth is that there's another voice constantly influencing every aspect of how you live your life—your subconscious—and it has more power over your behavior than you likely even know. Many times, it affects you in ways you don't even realize until someone points it out.

The subconscious operates largely in fear. It's your very own built-in defense mechanism, and it's always working. It remembers things you think you've long forgot, and the pain you've experienced throughout your life is its absolute favorite topic.

It uses that pain to protect you, which in some cases is a good thing. In others, it can act like a roadblock, keeping you from the life you should be living.

In my early adulthood, I became intensely fearful of flying. I was sure if I flew, I was going to die in a horrific accident. There was no basis for this fear I could pinpoint. I'd never had a bad experience flying. I certainly had never been in a crash or knew anyone who had. I'd never even so much as had to wait an inconvenient amount of time on a tarmac before takeoff. The fear of flying was completely devoid of reality. I would write long letters wishing my family goodbye and telling them how much I loved them and what I hoped for their future. I would close the letters in an envelope then seal them and label them "not to be opened until my death." It was insane.

I started asking myself, *Why am I so afraid of flying?* My job was requiring travel more and more, and this fear was starting to become a real problem. I would stay up all night before a flight. One day in a casual conversation, I told this to my mother, and she reminded me of a memory my mind had long since discarded.

When I was twelve years old, I was swinging on a rope attached to a tree. The rope snapped, and I fell about six feet, landing directly on my back onto an exposed tree trunk. At first, because I could barely move, everyone thought I had broken my back. It turned out I had sustained a severe friction burn on my back that was excruciating to the touch. For a long time afterward, I couldn't lay on my back. I barely slept for about a month.

That sensation of falling and the subsequent pain had stayed with me all those years and had manifested into my fear. It wasn't actually flying I was afraid of but rather the sensation of falling. It was never something I even thought about, but being on a plane and the subconscious thought of the falling sensation I'd experience when it would drop occasionally was triggering the fear I associated with falling from many years before. This also explained why I was afraid of rollercoasters.

Once I was able to pinpoint the root of my fear, I was able to overcome it simply by telling myself turbulence and small drops were all a part of the flying experience and nothing that could hurt me. I also did a ton of research on flying and finally convinced myself it was very safe compared to other things such as driving. My fear finally went away. Now, I fly with no problem. I actually like to sleep on a plane because now, my mind no longer associates it with a place of pain or fear.

EVERYTHING IS AFFECTED

If you've found yourself living a life that feels like less than what you were truly made for, chances are, you're just like I was—letting something in the background of your mind weigh on you until it stops you from moving forward. That scary moment, that failed relationship, that heartbreaking loss is creating a situation in which you're operating in avoidance of pain rather than in the pursuit of prosperity. It can affect you in ways both big and small. And likely, you don't even know this is happening in your life.

I once had an employee who was always showing up late. She was supposed to be at work by 8:00 a.m., and without fail, she showed up every day at 8:05. She always blamed traffic, so finally I suggested, "How about we move your start time back to 8:30?" Can you guess what happened? She started showing up at 8:35. I asked, "How are you still showing up late when I've given you an extra thirty minutes to get here?" She couldn't answer, but it's clear to me there is something in her subconscious mind that's making her self-sabotage. Perhaps she feels unworthy to have the job; perhaps she's not truly passionate about the work. Regardless of what it is, something in her subconscious mind is keeping her from arriving to work on time, and until she identifies what that is, she'll never overcome it and will likely never reach her true potential.

To do so will require her to look within and ask herself some tough questions, which she may not be willing to do. The tendency to want to avoid true introspection is the same reason so many people also suffer through one failed relationship after another. I've heard it said if you don't intentionally try to change the mind you had in the relationships you've had in the past, you will carry the same behaviors into any new relationship in the future. You won't even do it consciously. You'll get into the same arguments. You'll be annoyed by the exact same things. The reason nothing changes is because you haven't identified the things controlling your behavior. Until you recognize there are subconscious thoughts dictating your behaviors and shaping how you see the world, you will continue to repeat the same patterns and stay in the same place physically, mentally, emotionally, and spiritually.

There's no greater example of the subconscious's impact than how people feel about politics. In many cases, people believe what they believe based on something they don't even really comprehend. Most people can't say *why* they feel one way or another about an issue—they simply base their stance on an emotional reaction they're having to something they may have experienced earlier in life that's being driven by their subconscious.

Every move our subconscious leads us to make is done with one goal in mind: avoidance of future pain. And there's a certain type of pain that has a particularly strong staying power and a surefire way of keeping us from pursuing our heart's deepest hopes and dreams: shame and embarrassment.

RIDICULE AND THE SUBCONSCIOUS

Ridicule is a devaluation of one's worth as a human being. Our spirits hurt when other people don't see our value. It's one of the reasons people avoid criticism, constructive or otherwise. We all have a natural tendency to defend ourselves against anything that can harm us, whether physically, emotionally, or spiritually.

Ridicule—often a cruel form of criticism—leads to shame and embarrassment, which can scar us and cause us to become fearful. Fear exists to alert us to possible danger, and the reason we're fearful of ridicule is because it can destroy our spirit, just as it threatened to kill mine.

> RIDICULE IS A DEVALUATION OF
> ONE'S WORTH AS A HUMAN BEING.

STAGE FRIGHT

I have always loved to sing. Granted, I'm no Josh Groban or Michael Bublé but I can carry a tune. (Need I remind you of my aforementioned short-lived career as a member of a high school boy band?) But before I could work up the nerve to join that group or ever really sing in front of people at all, I had to overcome a debilitating fear of performing caused by the memory of one mean-spirited teacher I encountered during my elementary school days.

I'll preface this story with the reminder that I was in elementary school, and kids that young do things for no good reason. Therefore, I can't tell you why I was singing "The Star-Spangled

Banner" in the bathroom; I just was. And I wasn't humming—I was really belting it out, singing at the top of my lungs, happy and oblivious to the teacher who was listening just outside the bathroom door.

"Who's in there singing?" she snapped. I had no choice but to sheepishly show myself. She looked me up and down. "So, you like to sing?" she sneered. "You must, because we can hear you all the way in my class down the hallway." She pulled me down the hall and into her classroom, making me stand in front of rows of kids I didn't know. "Well? Go ahead!" she said, indicating the snickering audience. And she made me sing "The Star-Spangled Banner" right then and there.

I don't remember how many kids were in that classroom. I don't remember the teacher's name. The only thing I remember is what I felt when she made me sing: pure shame. Back then, things were a little different, but by today's standards, I'd say that teacher bullied me. She thought what she was doing was funny, a fitting punishment for disrupting her class. To me, it was the catalyst for years of being too terrified to sing or even speak in front of people.

To this day, it's very unlikely you will hear me sing in public. I sing quietly to myself in church. If I allow myself to sing in the car, it's only when I'm alone and certainly never when the windows are down. I even have trouble remembering the words to songs half the time. I can remember just about everything else: people's names, dates, quotes I've read and liked. But when it comes to songs, my brain just blocks out the words. I don't think about it consciously, but that elementary school experience is always in the back of my mind telling me that if I sing out loud, somebody's going to laugh. Somebody's going to ridicule me and I'll feel small and stupid. It was an experience that happened more than twenty-five years ago that continues to shape how I act today.

The effects of such experiences can impact far more than one's singing ability. When I first started dating my wife, Rachel, she'd often cook for me. When she asked, "How was it?" if I said anything less than, "It's great!" she'd get upset. If I made the mistake of saying, "It tastes really good," she would say, "Is it good or is it great?" If she pushed the issue and I dared to make a suggestion, something like, "I would love to have garlic bread with this spaghetti," it was game over. "You don't like anything I make," she'd say. "You just want to criticize me and put me down." Holy smokes! That escalated quickly.

Her reaction would throw me for a loop. It took this happening several times before I finally found out Rachel had been in a previous relationship with a verbally abusive guy. He called her names and would tell her she was worthless, that she was never going to achieve anything of value in life and she would be nothing without him. Fortunately, she got out of that relationship after just a few months, but the impact of his words was lasting. She was allowing her subconscious mind to dictate her emotional reaction. With its constant duty to protect her, Rachel's subconscious was telling her, *Here's somebody criticizing you. You have to react. You have to defend yourself.* She didn't even realize it until I pointed it out. She actually underwent counseling, which helped immensely, and now, instead of feeling instantly threatened, she can recognize when benign comments carry no intended harm to her well-being.

BLIND SPOTS

To different degrees, both mine and Rachel's experiences resulted in blind spots that caused us to behave a certain way with no clear reason in our minds as to why. We both were terrified of any kind of criticism. I did not want to be critiqued in any way because I remembered how it made me feel. I didn't want to do anything that put me in the spotlight.

Even well into my adulthood when I started to realize I had a passion to lead a business and engage in public speaking, I found myself resisting those goals. I was running away from the things I felt called to do because something I wasn't even aware of was controlling me. The ridicule from that moment all those years ago was keeping me from becoming the person I wanted to be. I didn't want to put myself out there. It was the same reason I never posted on Facebook or Instagram. I was terrified of anyone saying anything negative, but I had no idea why until I went to counseling when I was thirty-four years old.

It took some work, but I finally came to understand that terrible experiences had nothing to do with who I am now as a person. To help me move past it, my counselor encouraged me to write down all the things I felt were controlling me, then write a letter to a person who harmed me. One of the letters was to that teacher. I told my counselor I didn't know her name or anything about her. "It doesn't matter," he said. "Just tell her how you feel." I wrote: "Dear Teacher, When I was in fifth grade, you tried to take away my joy for singing. You tried to ridicule me. You tried to belittle me. Today, I'm a successful lawyer. I'm a great public speaker. I'm a great author. People want to know what I have to say. Despite your attempts to bring me down, I still became something, and you have no power over me." It felt so good, I decided to write letters to others who had wronged me: the coach who didn't give me a fair chance, the business partners who had dismissed me, anyone I felt had tried to hold me back. Then, I burned them all.

The act of writing the letters completely freed my mind of years of negativity it was carrying. Once I confronted the aspects of my subconscious that were holding me back, everything started falling into place. Now, I go through life feeling confident, valuable, and secure. I'm the managing partner of a successful firm. I have a consulting business that influences fifty thousand clients per year. I speak in public all the time. I fly often. Everything has changed because I dealt with the things that were holding me back. And best of all, I no longer find my value in what other people say or think of me, which has given me a much more freeing lifestyle.

REALITY BITES

Because no one can go through life without anything bad ever happening, we have to prepare ourselves to deal with harsh reality when it presents itself. It all starts by making a conscious effort to grow yourself as a person. As outlined in Chapter One, you have to begin to know and believe in who you are as an individual. The belief in yourself is key—without it, you won't be able to pursue the goals that will lead you to the life you're meant to live.

For instance, I heard a story of a woman who was amazing at baking cakes. She always toyed with the idea of opening her own bakery, but when it came time for her to charge a fair price for her cakes and the work she put into them, she couldn't do it. She'd say things like, "Nobody is going to pay $400 for a cake. Even though it took me twenty-five hours to build this elaborate custom-made cake, I'm selling it for $100." She couldn't bring herself to believe in her skills, and she ended up abandoning the bakery idea and taking a job in an unrelated field where she is utterly unfulfilled.

A few years later, a new bakeshop opened in town. It offered nearly the exact same cakes the woman did, but instead of short-changing themselves, the owners charged four times more than what she had. The place is still in business to this day and making money because the owners believe in their product and their talents.

Believing in yourself also makes you immune to ridicule or judgment. Because I believe I'm a great public speaker, it doesn't bother me when somebody says they don't like how I speak. I don't need an outside opinion to validate me. I've spent years working to become the speaker I am today, and I'm never going to worry about one bad review. In fact, after one of my speeches a few years ago, an older gentleman came to me and said, "Good effort." Clearly not a compliment. I still laugh about it today.

At the same time, you have to be able to recognize your own shortcomings and prepare to endure occasional criticism for them. I know I'm not a great lawyer—I am a much better businessman. Therefore, if somebody were to criticize me for not being a great lawyer, it would not affect me. Because I'm aware of my strengths and weaknesses, when somebody points out the latter, it only confirms what I already know. However, if someone said something negative about me as a business owner, it wouldn't affect me either. Not only does our $30 million business say otherwise, but beyond that, I believe in myself as a business owner and what others say can't make me question that. Once you know and believe in who you are, you simply don't accept any comments to the contrary. Your sense of self becomes unshakable.

BECAUSE NO ONE CAN GO THROUGH LIFE WITHOUT ANYTHING BAD EVER HAPPENING, WE HAVE TO PREPARE OURSELVES TO DEAL WITH HARSH REALITY WHEN IT PRESENTS ITSELF.

The next step in overcoming negativity is pinpointing the things in your subconscious that are holding you back. Once you identify the things that are limiting you, you have two options: continue to allow them to hold you back, or confront them and move on.

I found myself at such a crossroads when I looked at myself in the mirror one day and realized I had gained sixty-five pounds in about seven years and had no idea how or why. In my mind, none of my behaviors had changed. I wasn't eating more—or so I thought. But when I really took a step back and looked at how I was living my life, the reason for my weight gain wasn't such a mystery anymore.

When I was stressed, my go-to comfort was a king-size Reese's Peanut Butter Cup. I'd swing by the gas station, grab one and a bottle of Dr Pepper and enjoy my roughly six-hundred-calorie snack. Or, if I was on my way to court and I knew it was going to be stressful, I needed to make sure I had my Chick-fil-A meal with the four Chick-n-Minis and a big coffee with all the cream and sugar. I only ate when I was stressed—the problem was I was stressed all the time. I had to get control of these triggers. When I began to feel stressed, I made myself do something else like read, write, and go for a run. Since then, I lost sixty pounds and have kept it off to this day.

Just as I overcame my weight gain, my fear of flying, and my fear of public speaking, you, too, can confront the things holding you back and move past them to a happier, more prosperous future. The sooner you can become aware of the things that are controlling your actions, the sooner you can start taking steps to rectify your own behavior to ensure everything you do aligns with the life you want for yourself.

CHAPTER TWO EXERCISES

To pinpoint the fears that are holding you back and learn how to work around them, ask five of your closest family members and friends the following three questions:

- What am I good at doing?
- Where am I limiting myself?
- What causes me to react negatively?
- Where do I seem to constantly be stuck?

Give them the freedom to be honest, and be ready to experience some discomfort because the answers will show you how fear is keeping you from the future you are meant for.

CHAPTER THREE

HATERS, BAITERS, AND IMPERSONATORS

DEALING WITH THOSE WHO WANT TO HOLD YOU BACK

"I repeat, you are the only you there is and ever will be. Do not deny the world its one and only chance to bask in your brilliance."

—JEN SINCERO

As you work toward self-improvement, a certain group of people are going to emerge in ways you've never noticed before: haters, baiters, and impersonators. These people are tough. Worse yet, many times they don't even know you. These are the people who simply cannot see the vision you have for yourself—in fact, they aren't even interested in trying to see it. For whatever reason, likely something deeply personal that's more a reflection of how they feel about themselves than how they feel about you, they want to keep you exactly where you are, and they will say and do just about anything to do so. What I have learned over time is that all too often, insecure people want to project their insecurities onto you. The worst part is you might not even be aware they are doing it. *They* might not even be aware they're doing it. But you still will have to learn to recognize this quality in the people in your life and decide how you want to deal with it.

My first experience with a hater came in high school, during a period of upheaval in my life. I was entering ninth grade and had just moved to the States from Puerto Rico. My dad had joined the military, and we found out one week before school was set to start, he'd be stationed in New Jersey. We packed up all our bags, spent three months in Jersey, then set off for Georgia, where I was eager to get settled and join the school's baseball team.

Having already played baseball for a few years by that point, I was hoping to become a starter in my freshman year. I made the JV team as a shortstop, but a finger fracture sustained during a practice meant I couldn't throw as far, and I was moved to second base. Despite that, I got called up to the varsity team and was a reliable pinch runner.

Based on my performance my freshman year, I started tenth grade feeling pretty confident about my chances of getting some quality playing time. However, there was another player in the second base position—none other than the coach's son.

I knew I was never going to play. The coach's son was also a great hitter, ending up with ten home runs per year and that, of course, was an important asset. But none of that mattered. I could have been an all-pro. He was a coach's son; he was going to play. At least that's how *I* felt.

Granted, I could have transitioned back to shortstop, but by now I had spent two seasons playing second base. I didn't want to give that up, which meant I spent a lot of time on the bench.

The hardest part was that I wasn't even being given a shot. Any opportunity I'd hoped to have for myself was taken away. I was beyond frustrated, and so was my dad. Unbeknownst to me, he was so upset, he sent a letter to the coaches saying he thought it was unfair I was not being given a shot to play. And as I'd come to find out, his letter was not at all well received.

I was sitting in class one day when I was called to talk to one of the coaches. Still not knowing anything about my dad's letter, I had no idea what the coach wanted. He sat me down and said, "Look, I know you think you're better than the guys who are starting on the field. I know you think it's unfair that you're not playing, but the truth is, you're not a starter. You're not as good as him, and we don't think you have the capability he has. You're not as consistent as him." He proceeded to give me a laundry list of reasons why I shouldn't be given a chance, why I wasn't as good as the coach's son, and why I wasn't going to be able to play the position. He ended by saying, "I hope you understand."

To me, this conversation was beyond bizarre. I had never said a word to anyone on the team about this. I had always hustled. I had always worked hard. Yes, I thought I should get a chance, but I hadn't gone around complaining to anyone. I was frustrated, but I was still confident, and I knew I would get my chance—it was just a matter of time. So, this conversation was a bit surprising.

I went home that day and told my dad, "This is going to sound really strange but today, the coach pulled me out of class to tell me I wasn't any good." My dad became furious. He thought the coach understood he'd sent that letter man-to-man. He had no intention of me even knowing about it. But when he told me what he did, everything made sense. If you're a coach and your son is on your team, you're probably not going to be too happy some other parent is saying you shouldn't play your own kid. Most parents are defensive of their kids even when they are terrible at something; at least my coach knew his son was good. And he was not going to simply agree with my dad's letter and give me the playing time I thought I deserved based on one letter.

While I understand all of that in retrospect, at the time, the coach's message of "You're not good enough" created a crossroads in my life. I could have decided to take it to heart, quit the team, and never touch a baseball again. Instead, I decided I was going to continue to believe in my capabilities. I started coming to practice early and staying late. I worked out on the weekends and improved my running. I hustled even harder. I ate, slept, and breathed baseball. I did everything I could possibly do to make myself the absolute best player I could be. And after all that, I got a scholarship to play Division 1 baseball even though I only started at second base one season in my senior year (with a torn ACL on top of it all, don't forget).

It was a personal victory for me. The entire experience developed in me an insatiable desire to prove people wrong. To this day, if anyone says I can't do something, I do it. For better or worse, it made me the intensely competitive person I am now.

I say all of this knowing now that no one in this scenario had bad intentions. They all thought they were trying to help. They were accidental diminishers—they weren't even aware of the impact they were having on me. They clearly thought the other player was better, and maybe in tenth grade, I wasn't as good. It took me years to accept this and be able to get past it. But fortunately for me, this experience fueled me to become the person I am today.

THE DANGER OF HATERS

Haters are crushers of dreams. I believe some of the best inventions have never been invented because of haters. Some of the greatest recipes have never been tasted because of haters. Too many amazing talents have never been given the chance to shine because of the control we give to the haters in our lives.

When you let a hater have any kind of control over your life, you're putting your future, your greatness, and your calling into the hands of someone who does not have to live with the outcome of your decisions. They have no real stake in the game. It would be like having children simply because someone else told you that you should. That person is not going to raise those kids—you are. They made the choice for you but have no responsibility for the outcome. When you let a hater dictate your action (or inaction), you end up living a life that's not truly your own. You end up letting someone live rent-free in your mind. And today is the day to evict them.

You are ultimately responsible for the success of your life. Ralph Waldo Emerson, in his essay regarding the Law of Compensation, says, "As long as all that is said is said against me, I feel a certain assurance of success. But as soon as honeyed words of praise are spoken of me, I feel as one that lies unprotected before his enemies." I believe he is saying we must use the negative to fuel us while being careful the positive does not give us so much pride that we become susceptible to those who oppose us.

While entrusting such people with the decisions of your life is clearly destructive, it happens all the time. Many people live a life someone else tells them to live because they lack the confidence to do otherwise. I could have believed the coach who pulled me out. But I didn't. Yet so many dreams have been shattered because of this negativity, which is the true danger of allowing haters to control you. You end up living a life that doesn't carry the significance you want. It doesn't involve any of the accomplishments or achievements you dreamed about, and yet such a fate could have been totally avoided. You could have overcome all of it had you just tuned out haters and instead listened to your own heart and followed your own dreams.

Think of what the world would be like if everyone who encountered a hater let them win. I can only imagine how many times Facebook founder Mark Zuckerberg heard things like, "That is the dumbest idea I've ever heard of. Why would anybody want to connect like that?" People who are not visionaries are never going to be able to see your vision. Why would you let someone like that control your thought process and dictate how you're going to live your life?

HATERS ARE CRUSHERS OF DREAMS.

I've encountered many haters in my life. I once visited a friend who was attending law school in another city. I was starting law school soon as well, and he asked me about my plans. I told him I was going to go to Atlanta's John Marshall Law School. He said, "Man, why would you go to *that* school? That's like a third-tier school. You're not even going to be able to find a job with that school. You're not going to be able to practice. Are you even going to pass the bar? You need to go to a more prestigious school."

Then he added: "You should apply to other schools. You're a minority. You'll get in no problem. It'll be so easy for you."

In one conversation, he told me I was making the dumbest decision of my life going to a third-tier school, and if I decided to go somewhere better, the only reason I would get in was because I was a minority. I let that weigh on the back of my mind for some time. I wondered if I really was making a huge mistake. However, I didn't let his words change my plans. I knew what I wanted, I knew how I wanted to get it, and in the end, everything worked out fine. Now I run an eight-figure law firm with 150 employees and am called upon all over the country to help other people build their own firms.

It's truly amazing how people will try to influence you, even when they do not always mean harm. He probably never said those things to hurt me. He was honestly trying to help. But regardless of his intention in that situation, he ended up coming off as just another person who didn't want me to succeed. A lot of people think they know better than you and feel some need to "impart their wisdom" to you. They do all this not realizing that what they're actually doing is hurting you emotionally, spiritually, or mentally.

One way to avoid all of this negativity is to be careful when choosing who you share your goals with. Unfortunately, there are too many people out there who are not really there to encourage you to accomplish all you want in life. It helps to identify these haters and save talking about your dreams for the people in your life who genuinely want to see you succeed.

MY ULTIMATE HATER EXPERIENCE

Being told I wasn't good enough to play baseball sparked the fire of my competitive spirit. Being told I made a mistake going to the law school I chose fanned the flames. The dissolution of my business partnership ignited a raging blaze.

I had joined the business, a law firm, in 2004. When I was hired, the firm had three employees, and I became a jack-of-all-trades. I was hired as a part-timer to cover for an employee who was going to Europe for one month. Eventually, I did paralegal work. I did legal assistant work. I did interpreting jobs. I net-worked. I did marketing. Basically, I did everything I could to help the business succeed.

During my time there and thanks largely to my efforts, the business grew dramatically. We grew from three people up to twenty-four employees, and our revenue climbed into seven figures in a short amount of time. With my ability for networking and generating business and ultimately revenue, I knew I wanted to own and run a law firm of my own. For years, people told me to start my own business, but I was loyal and committed to the firm and did not want to leave. So, I went to law school and continued to grind as hard as I could. At the end of law school, it was becoming clear I would have to become a partner simply because otherwise, I would end up starting my own firm.

Yet it wasn't a move the other two partners were terribly excited about. I was fifteen to twenty years younger than them. I had different ideas for the future of the firm than they did. At the time, I was focused on my leadership abilities. I was realiz-ing I had a great knack for managing the business end of things, and in my mind, that meant I had to stop practicing law and turn my full attention to operations. They agreed to let me do this, and I got busy developing the marketing department and the sales intake department, finding interns to work for us and even hiring another lawyer.

I began to sense resentment. In their mind, I wasn't *really* working. I wasn't in the courtroom. I was moving numbers around and costing them money. I was flying off to conferences and having a great time. What they couldn't understand was that while I was doing all those things, not only was I missing time with my family, but I was learning how to build a success-ful business. I wanted to *build* a law business while they wanted to *run* a law practice, and this misalignment in vision caused everything to start breaking down.

In January 2018, four years after we started working together as partners, they came to me and said they wanted to terminate the partnership. But the way they did it was what hurt the most. They said, "We are terminating the partnership and restarting a partnership with you excluded. We will keep all the cases and employees, the name, and the website and all of the assets you helped accumulate. We will pay you a 'fair' amount for all of it." What they really were telling me was that they didn't see any value in my leadership. I had made it clear to them the vision I had for myself and the firm. With the termination, they were responding with a firm and final "no" to my vision. It was shocking and disappointing because I felt they did not see my value and worth. There are always two sides to every story, and I'm sure they had their reasons, but the loss of the partnership—the relationship I thought I was going to have for the next twenty years—doesn't sting any less.

In that moment, I rose from my chair and left. I didn't complain. I didn't argue. I didn't ask why or demand they reconsider. I simply got up, left the office, went home, showered, put on a fresh suit, and went to a networking meeting that afternoon.

That day, I decided I was going to start a competing law firm and began looking for space. One month later, I signed the dissolution papers. One week after that, I announced the launch of my own firm. Through a series of incredible fortune and blessings, my law firm shot out of a cannon bringing on one hundred clients in the first five months as well as five employees. Then through a joint venture two years later, my business was on track to generate $30 million in revenue.

Looking back, I credit my previous experience with my coach for giving me the resolve to handle the dissolution of my partnership. I had been there before—I had been told I couldn't do something, and I still did it. I knew I would do it again. I wanted to prove my former partners wrong the same way I wanted to prove my coach wrong. Again, I relied on my support system—my parents—to help me through when I needed it. And again, I made it through, stronger for having endured the hardship created by people who told me all the reasons why what I wanted would never work.

You, too, are going to have haters in your life. There's nothing you can do to prevent it. All you can do is prepare yourself to handle them as best as you can.

SHUTTING DOWN HATERS

To do battle with a hater, you have to have a strong sense of who you are as a person. You have to be sure in your own identity (starting to sound familiar?) because only by understanding yourself at the highest possible level can you avoid faltering when haters attack.

Part of knowing your identity is recognizing the things that trigger you to give up. For a while, I was triggered any time I sensed opposition. I also had imposter syndrome. I felt I wasn't qualified enough to be a speaker or a consultant or a good lawyer. As explored in Chapter Two, you have to look into your subconscious to figure out what's holding you back, then make sure you have control over it before haters can tap into those insecurities and feed them with their own negativity. Other people who know you will make their own assumptions about your blind spots—don't give them the opportunity to use those weaknesses to wield power over you. If you already know what drives you subconsciously, no one else can use that against you.

After that, it's just a matter of believing you are somebody special. Because you absolutely are. It may seem easier said than done, but the simple truth is you cannot deny the world its one and only chance to bask in your brilliance. You have to start believing you are amazing. You have to start recognizing the fact that you were intended for more. You have to start believing you are great. There is no question you have something about you that makes you special—we all do. Once you figure out what that is and own it, no one can take that away.

All of this will require you to rise above the negativity. Negative people are like a contagious cancer. They spread their negativity through you and through others. They destroy your mindset and steal your joy. They tear you down because they don't want to face the fact they are not rising to their own potential. I once heard a saying that oftentimes, people will see you taking big strides toward following your dream and call you irresponsible, selfish, or insane. They do that because they've convinced themselves they can't chase their own goals, and they believe those things about themselves. All of us spend so much time around mediocre people who have convinced themselves they cannot achieve their dreams. They are going to be negative. They are going to hold you back. They're going to try to prevent you from doing anything of value with your life, because they don't want to come face-to-face with the reality that they have never achieved anything. Most people who are negative toward you have never accomplished anything in their lives. Most successful people applaud the accomplishments of others rather than work to tear others down. When I see a person being negative about others, I know they are either not successful or projecting their own insecurity.

In some extreme cases, the only answer is to cut that person out of your life. But some of these people likely will be family who you can't remove completely. You might be experiencing this with your spouse. Maybe it's your adult children. Maybe it's a coworker or a boss. If your hater is someone who plays a key role in your life, you'll have to learn to either ignore their negativity or find a way to make it known that you can no longer continue with the relationship the way it is and work on establishing boundaries moving forward. If, however, your hater is someone who holds less priority in your life, I'd suggest simply limiting your exposure to them.

An easy place to start is by weeding haters out of your social media feeds. Social media is a breeding ground for negativity, and we consume it all day long. Then, we wonder why we don't have a more positive outlook. I've learned this firsthand again and again (and again) as I've worked over the last few years to grow my social media following. I can tell you no matter what you post, no matter how benign or positive it may seem, *someone* will find a way to make it negative. I once posted a selfie with a caption asking my followers to take a serious look at themselves and think about what they are doing to better their own lives. One commenter (notice I'm being nice with "commenter" and not the more appropriate "troll") had this observation to share: "Dude, you have some big ass eyeballs." Hey, thanks, random stranger. Super relevant. But instead of letting that negativity just hang out there, I responded, as I usually do to such people. I said, "I never really noticed that. Thanks for pointing it out!" I never let their negativity drag me down. Most people never reengage, and that just goes to show all they were doing is trying to be hateful. On social media, you just have to accept that negativity is coming and learn to see it for what it is: nasty people being nasty. And if you follow someone who's only putting negativity on their feed, unfollow. Do not let their posts poison you anymore.

OWNING YOUR EMPOWERMENT

There is nothing you can do to prevent haters from appearing in your life, because there simply are too many people who are so down about their own situations, they have nothing positive to offer. No one can give something they don't have. Unfortunately, you're going to encounter such people at every level of your life, whether you're just starting to work on yourself or you're living the fulfilling life you always wanted. This means you have to maintain your strong sense of self so as you continue on your journey, no hater ever becomes a roadblock on your path to success.

Ultimately, you should be empowered to create the life you deserve to have. You should be empowered because you deserve to have it, and those around you deserve to have the best of you. Every once in a while, I like to ask my employees this question: "Do you deserve my best?" What I mean by that is do they deserve my coming in every day and having a great attitude? Do they deserve my treating them with respect and dignity? Do they deserve my being open and transparent with them? Do they deserve my creating opportunities for them to succeed?

They always answer yes. And I reply, "Well, if you deserve my best, don't I deserve yours?" I ask this because there are some people who come to work and expect the best from others but are not willing to give the best of themselves. Everyone should to be empowered to create the lives they deserve both for themselves and to help others have the lives they deserve as well. You can't let haters keep you from giving your best to the world. When you let someone tell you that you can't start a restaurant, you can't hit your goal weight, you can't make the money you want, you can't have the car or the house you want, you're letting them keep you from your best and possibly depriving others who deserve your best from experiencing it. Rather than letting a hater tell you what you can't do, I encourage you to focus on being excited about what you can do. Yes, there might be some truth to what a hater is telling you because life will not always be easy. You're going to experience hardship no matter what. Why not view those experiences as a way to help you become the best version of yourself possible rather than letting the fear of them hold you back?

There is nothing better than becoming who you were meant to be and living in that authenticity. When you reach that state, haters can never have control over your values or actions. Because the truth is your character is not defined by what people say about you; your character is defined by what you do *despite* what people say about you. It's defined by all the times you show up early. It's defined by all the times you stay late. It's the times you do that extra rep in the gym or run that extra mile. It's the times you save that dollar to put toward your dream instead of indulging in something you don't need. It's that new book you read. It's the time you invest in yourself. Haters can try to control you emotionally and mentally by saying you can't do something, but they never can control your actions—unless you let them.

THERE IS NOTHING BETTER THAN BECOMING WHO YOU WERE MEANT TO BE AND LIVING IN THAT AUTHENTICITY.

PLAN OF ATTACK

When people in your life are being negative, you have two choices: prove them right or prove them wrong. Doing the latter requires a plan. First, ask yourself in a clear and concrete way what it is you want to achieve. Make your answer as specific as possible. Don't just say, "I want to make more money." Say, "I want to make $100,000 a year." Write it down and think about exactly what needs to happen for you to make that goal a reality. Understand it's not going to happen overnight. Think about everything it will require of you. How many mentors are you going to talk to? How many books are you going to read? How many conferences are you going to go to? How many coaching sessions are you going to have? What are you going to do to develop yourself into the person the haters said you couldn't become?

Now is the time to conquer the triggers that keep you from executing the plan. It's easy to put a plan into writing; putting it into action is a whole new ball game. When you start committing to action, you run the risk of being hurt or disappointed and not achieving. You have to figure out a way to stop avoiding disappointments and bounce back when they inevitably occur. One thing I do to bounce back is remind myself that disappointments are just a part of life. Everyone is disappointed at some point, and the most important part of disappointment is the response you have to it. It's up to you if it's positive or negative. I encourage you to make it positive by using it to fuel future success—easier said than done, to be sure, but well worth it in the long run.

Once you have a concrete plan in place, all you have to do is stay the course. Do not allow giving up to be an option, ever. Simply remove it as a possibility in your mind. Too many people give up before they give themselves an opportunity to succeed. Remember, the greatest indicator of your true desire is action. Inaction is a way of letting the haters win. Just letting their negative words roll off your back isn't enough—you have to put yourself into action and prove them wrong. You have to actually do something to change the trajectory of your life.

When you fail to act, you're showing the world you do not care about becoming the person you are supposed to be.

INTENTION ISN'T ENOUGH

The journey to obtaining all the things you want in life begins with a change within you—not a change in your haters, your job, your living situation, your friends, your family, or your finances. Everything starts with you. No one will value you more than you value yourself. If you believe you are only worth minimum wage, you will only ever make minimum wage. If you believe the opinions of others matter more than what you think of yourself, you will base your life on what others expect of you. If you believe life is always out to hold you back, you will let life hold you back.

As you begin your journey, it's crucial to keep in mind the fact that personal growth precedes professional growth. If you truly want to create the lifestyle you've always dreamed of, you must begin to believe you're worth more, and the only way to do that is to figure out how to create more value in yourself. The more you grow as a person, the more valuable you become as a person and the more you begin to believe in yourself. The more you begin to believe in yourself, the more value you create for others, and the more value you create for others, the more successful you'll be.

Overcoming all the things that previously held you back will require all of your effort; intention is not enough. What you need now is action. You can't just *intend* to create more value. You can't intend to read more books. You can't intend to go to the gym. You can't intend to block out the haters. You can't intend to do anything—you have to actually *do* it. Because in the end, action is the greatest evidence of your true desire. The things you say, the things you think, the things you *want to do* aren't what really matters. Your actions matter most.

If you say you want to lose weight but don't go to the gym, eat healthy, drink enough water, or get enough sleep, your actions are proving you are not committed to that goal. In fact, the action of not doing those things is evidence you don't really want to lose weight at all. If you did, you would take action. Simple as that. This applies to any goal, whether it's getting a promotion or a new job, reading more, getting a degree, anything. You can say you want something again and again, but action will prove whether or not that's actually true. When I went to law school, I worked a full-time job forty to fifty hours a week. I had to get up early in the morning and stay up late. I got home at 10:00 p.m. most nights and was up by 6:30 a.m. most mornings. I did that for almost four years until I got my degree and passed the bar exam. It wasn't fun, but my action was the evidence of my true desire to become a lawyer.

Furthermore, when you say you want something but aren't willing to take action, it can be harmful to your mind and spirit because ultimately, you're only disappointing yourself. And there's no harsher critic of your life than you. When you become a disappointment to yourself, you begin to lose hope that anything is possible for the future. The voice in your head starts saying, *You've let me down so many times. You've given up so many times. You've stopped working out so many times. You've given up on your business. You've quit on the dream. I have no confidence you're going to be able to do this again.* You become your own hater.

If this sounds all too familiar, know you're not alone. Many of us wish people would judge us on our intentions. We all want others to believe we have a good heart, because we convince ourselves that will be enough. We tell ourselves, "It doesn't matter that I've lied, cheated, stolen, been disrespectful, or haven't treated people right. I have a good heart, and therefore I'm a good person." And as long as we accept the idea that intention is enough, we don't have to do anything. We don't have to experience risk. We don't have to go through the pain of life. But the truth is people don't judge each other on their intentions—our judgments are based on action.

The reason so many people get stuck on intention is because it's easy. It's easy to wake up and say, "Today, I intend to go to the gym. Today, I to intend to pay down some credit card debt. Today, I intend to start a business. Today, I intend to write a book." It's a thousand times harder to actually get up and go to the gym, make that payment, work on that business, or start writing. But without action, nothing ever gets accomplished, and you remain stuck, only wishing life would hand you the things you claim to want.

I've been there. In the past, I've written thirteen books, none of them published until now. Before this book, it was easy for me to write and not pursue publishing because there was no risk. Nobody had to read what I wrote. I didn't have to confront the possibility of people not liking my book. I didn't have to worry about putting my book on Amazon and getting a two-star rating. But action requires courage, so I had to muster all that I had and just go for it. Intention requires no courage, no risk. Nobody criticizes you for intention. Countless times, I've asked people in my business about their goals and dreams. Many say they want to be a lawyer. That's their intention. It sounds good. They can go to a cocktail party, tell people, "I plan to go to law school," and everyone at that party is going to assume they are successful because they have such a big dream. But are they actively pursuing this goal with action?

What I have found is that when I ask that same person, "So,

what are you doing to pursue that goal?" the answer is often the same: "Well, I work at a law firm right now, but I'm going to go to law school." That's a lie they could tell for ten years, and nobody would ever know. Never mind the fact that they've never taken the law school entry exam. Never mind the fact that they had a 2.5 GPA during their undergraduate studies. Never mind the fact that they've never taken any positive steps toward actually becoming a lawyer. It sounds so good to just say they're going to be a lawyer, there's no need to actually make it a reality.

People also get stuck in intention because it is rewarded in our society. Intention always is applauded whereas actually reaching a goal can invite negativity. For example, if you tell people you want to lose weight, they will cheer you on. They'll offer all kinds of encouragement and positivity. Yet as soon as you do lose the weight, they'll become haters and look for reasons to undermine your accomplishment: "Well, what kind of diet were you on? You must have starved yourself. You must not have to work that hard because you have a good metabolism. I have a bad metabolism." They won't take into account all the sacrifice, the exercise, the hard work you had to do to get the results you wanted. Had you stayed stuck on intention, most likely no one ever would have questioned how you planned to accomplish your goal. They would have kept encouraging you because intention is always cheered on and requires no risk. But overcoming negativity and truly tapping into who you are meant to be requires a great deal of it.

Don't let your haters hold you back. Make the decision today to be great.

CHAPTER THREE EXERCISES

To identify the haters in your life and begin to move past them, ask yourself:

- Who in your life is actively bringing you down? Do they know they're diminishing you?
- How can you teach them to be a promoter instead of a detractor?
- How can you avoid people who intentionally bring you down?
- What do you have to do to find more encouragers in your life?

CHAPTER FOUR

BE GREAT BY BEING YOU

FINDING YOUR PASSION AND EMBRACING THE PERSON YOU ARE MEANT TO BE

"You must expect great things of yourself before you can do them."

—MICHAEL JORDAN

Have you ever thought you were made for more despite the haters in your life or any other negativity you're experiencing? Have you ever felt as if something was nagging at your heart telling you you're not currently the person you were meant to be? Are you going to work all day in a daze, only to come home and wonder how your life became so mundane? Are you asking yourself, "Is this it?" while secretly suspecting there has to be something greater waiting for you?

When you just know you're meant for more but just not sure *what*, you are on what I call "the treadmill of life." I was on that same treadmill for longer than I care to admit. It didn't matter how much money I made. It didn't matter what job I had. I kept making more and more money; I kept getting promotion after promotion, yet I still felt like I wasn't advancing in any way. I felt stuck because while I was seemingly doing all the right things, I wasn't doing what I was truly meant to be doing. I wasn't activating the seed of greatness inside of me, and until I did, nothing would ever be enough. But then I decided to be great.

There are seeds of greatness in each one of us. Every single person on this planet has something inside of them that makes them amazing. But the reason this book is titled *It Has to Hurt* is because achieving that seed of greatness many times requires us to work harder than we ever imagined and endure challenges we never could anticipate. Many people never give themselves the time to develop their seeds of greatness, opting instead to dwell on doubt, asking themselves again and again, *Am I even worth more?* The question they should be asking, however, is, *What value can I bring to people?* The second question is rooted in the understanding that you are worth more. You should already know you are capable of greatness—you just need to discover how you can best share that with the world. But doubt is a powerful crusher of dreams, and to even tap into your seeds of greatness, you will have to learn to push past it at all costs.

THERE ARE SEEDS OF GREATNESS IN EACH ONE OF US.

SELF-LIMITING BELIEFS

The most common things holding people back from understanding their own worth are self-limiting beliefs. Many people are raised in environments where they are not taught that they can achieve greatness. Instead, they embrace the idea that settling for complacency is acceptable. When you live like this, you tend to look at others who are achieving and instead of seeing it as motivation to better yourself, you allow yourself to feel like a victim. Social media feeds this, as you see everyone on vacation, eating at classy restaurants, having a great time with their spouses, hiking, camping, running marathons, *living*. Such information has a profound impact on you, especially when you're well into adulthood. You might look at that and think, *I'm thirty-five. That guy is twenty-six and he just ran an Iron Man. He went to Bali for his honeymoon. He just bought his first house.* If you're a single guy in his thirties who's never worked out a day in his life, that's likely going to enrage you more than motivate you. Instead of thinking, *That could be me!* you'll think, *Man, it sucks that could never be me.* You assign a limitation to your own life, and the only way to overcome it is by beginning to believe in what is great inside of you, not the snapshots of another's life you're seeing online.

So many people *say* they want that nice car, big house, good job, huge paycheck, great relationship, killer body, but they don't really *believe* they can have it. I'm guilty of this. For ages, I talked about how much I wanted six-pack abs. I worked out but when, after months of dedicated gym time, I saw no six-pack emerge, my belief in my ability to coax them out faltered big time. When I finally saw Peyton Manning in a commercial saying, "You want abs like this? Well, unless you're an NFL football player or a teenager, you're not going to have them," it was all I needed to hear to give up the dream.

So many of us set out to accomplish something great, then when we try for a short time and don't immediately achieve results, we give up. And the reason we give up is self-limiting belief. We start to believe the voice in our head that tells us we can't do something. Though sometimes, it's not even the voice in your head. Sometimes, it's Peyton Manning.

SELF-DOUBT

Self-doubt is different from self-limiting beliefs. Self-limiting beliefs keep us from working out as hard as we can at the gym; self-doubt keeps us from even getting off the couch long enough to change into our gym clothes. When you doubt yourself, it can keep you from believing anything is ever worth trying.

Self-doubters are the people who hate their jobs but do nothing to change them. They're in crappy relationships and stay in them for far too long (or sometimes, forever). They scrape by financially and complain about their low paychecks to anyone who will listen. Yet these same people never even attempt to improve or change their situations because they truly believe nothing better awaits them. Their seeds of greatness are doomed to remain dormant unless they make some drastic changes.

When I first had the feeling that I was made to be a public speaker, I couldn't believe it. I firmly doubted I could actually do it. *Nobody really wants to hear me speak*, I'd think. *I have nothing to offer people. This is never going to happen.* And for a long time, nothing did. Then I got asked to speak at a few events, and I started thinking, *Okay, sure. They asked me to speak, but it's not going to be in front of many people, and they definitely are not going to pay me for it.* Then I got a gig speaking in front of 1,500 people. I thought, *Yeah, but nobody's going to book me again.* My self-doubt wouldn't even let me believe I could do it when I was *already doing it*. Eventually, I had to acknowledge that the way I was thinking and feeling was just wrong. There was too much evidence to the contrary. I destroyed my own self-doubt by doing the very thing I was convinced I couldn't.

It was because of this self-doubt that I spent many years not even pursuing the goal of public speaking. I never crafted a signature talk, I never reached out to any event organizers, and

I never worked on perfecting my craft. I had too much doubt that it was even possible for me.

MISSED OPPORTUNITIES

Many people fail to act on the opportunities life presents them because they let fear keep them from even exploring what might be possible. My dad likes to say, "If opportunity knocks, you enter," meaning you open the door and walk through it. I once asked him, "How do you know if it's a good opportunity to enter into?"

"Simple. You always enter," he said.

"Right, but what if it's a bad opportunity?" I asked.

"If it's a bad opportunity, you have to have faith that the door will close on you and you won't have to worry about it," he said.

I have found those words to be extremely true. In college, when I made the decision to go to a different school, opportunity came knocking. I applied to go to Columbus State, West Georgia, and Valdosta State and got a tryout for each school's baseball team. I walked through all three school doors. I went to the interviews and to the tryouts for each. I was *certain* I was going to get picked up by Columbus State—the school I most wanted to attend as it was closest to where my parents lived—but they didn't offer me a scholarship. Even though it was what I thought I wanted, that door was closed.

As a backup, I planned to attend Valdosta State but at the last moment, West Georgia offered me a better opportunity. With that, the Valdosta State door closed and the West Georgia door opened. I accepted the scholarship and ended up playing three more years of baseball. Had I not let myself be open to the opportunities being presented to me, none of that ever would have happened.

I later found myself in a similar situation in my career. I already had started my own law firm and had been up and running for about five months when opportunity came knocking again. The person who would become my partner approached me multiple times, saying, "Hey, let's work together." At first, I wasn't so certain this was a door I should enter.

But the words of my father rang loudly in my mind, and I decided to meet with him. That initial two-hour meeting turned into a twelve-hour meeting. That twelve-hour meeting turned into a four-day trip during which we talked about nothing but the business we hoped to run. That four-day trip turned into me becoming employed with him the next week. That employment turned into me developing a business plan, and that plan turned into me becoming a partner. As of this writing, we've grown our business from twenty-five employees to almost 150. And it's all because of my father's advice to always be open to opportunity. Had I not taken his words to heart, I never would have made the decision to move forward with this partnership.

Too many people miss the opportunity. They miss it because they're fearful. They miss it because other people are negative to them. They miss it because they don't want to take the risk. They miss it because they wait too long to make a good decision. All of this prevents people from activating their own seed of greatness, but the good news is you are in control of how you choose to respond to opportunity. Even if you do miss an opportunity, you can turn that experience into a positive by learning from it and using it to inform who you truly are supposed to be. When you do that, a missed opportunity is nothing more than a detour; you're still on the road to achieving that which you are supposed to achieve. The most important thing, in any scenario, is to take action, because without action, nothing will be possible.

GIVE UP ON GIVING UP

When you allow quitting to be an option, you all but guarantee it's the option you'll choose. It's the reason so many people give up right before their goals are reached. If I ever find myself feeling tempted to quit, I always think of the Israelites in the desert. They spent forty years in the desert looking for the Promised Land. What would have happened if they would have given up in year thirty-nine? Yet so many bail at the last minute because it's easier to give up than to keep searching. It's easier to not become who you were meant to be than to constantly feel as if all your perseverance is not paying off. The pain of perseverance sometimes feels heavier than the price of quitting, but I have found the pain of regret from quitting will always be greater.

It is the same reason why so many restaurants fail. Owners open their doors and do well in years one and two, but if they're not raking in amazing profits by years three or four, they close. They don't realize much more time is needed to establish a successful business and rather than weathering the rough years, they bow out and abandon their dream. They also may not have planned correctly and may not have enough cash or the right marketing plan to make the money to stay open.

Granted, it is important to be able to recognize when there genuinely is no hope for the situation. If you've exhausted every possibility and walking away from a goal is the only reasonable course of action, I'm not suggesting you stay invested simply to be able to say you did. But in most situations, people give up before getting to that point, and when they do, they limit their opportunity to activate their own seed of greatness.

**WHEN YOU ALLOW QUITTING TO BE
AN OPTION, YOU ALL BUT GUARANTEE
IT'S THE ONE YOU'LL CHOOSE.**

FEAR OF JUDGMENT

In my book club, we talk about a lot more than just books. During one meeting, I posed the question: if you could be or do anything in this world, what would it be? Each person gave their response. And then each person said they could never do what they really wanted because of someone in their life who wouldn't understand why they were doing it.

One woman answered right away: "If I could do anything in my life right now, I would move to the beach." She had clearly thought this through. She talked about how much she would love to see the ocean every day and get a job in tourism. She'd probably live in a smaller home and make less money, but her life would be much less stressful and would be filled with the things she genuinely cared about. Listening to her speak so passionately, I said, "Get up and go! What could possibly be holding you back from living that life?"

"Well," she said quietly. "My parents would be so upset. They'd say I'm wasting my life."

The woman was so scared of what her parents might say about her dream, she would never even allow herself to consider it a real possibility. She, like so many others, was terrified of judgment. Worse yet, she was forty years old and scared of what her parents thought. Unfortunately, it is a harsh reality that when you start to articulate your dreams, people are going to have opinions. They're going to perceive it as too crazy, too risky, or just plain dumb. They're going to insinuate you're shirking responsibility, not doing what you're "supposed" to be doing, going against what the world requires of you.

There are always going to people who, when presented with your dreams, are confronted with their own mediocrity and instinctively, they're going to look for ways to bring you down. Because the real meaning behind their comments is, "Don't make an attempt to succeed—just stay here and be a failure with me." Remember, a person who's not a visionary is never going to be able to see your vision. Someone incapable of thinking as big as you will never view the world the way you do. And to let a person like that hold you back is absurd. You have to accept the fact that as you pursue your dreams, you are going to be confronted with dozens (or even, if you're lucky, thousands) of absolute losers who do not want you to be successful.

When somebody imposes a judgment on you, it's always more of a reflection of how they see themselves. They are speaking from a place of disappointment in themselves for the choices they've made in the past and fear of what they'd have to do to change their life in the future. Their negativity has *nothing to do with you*; it has everything to do with them. It's rooted in their own experiences, their own context, and their own points of reference.

If you're going to share a dream, you have to expect that people are going to say negative things. Just remember it's not what they say about you that matters; it's what you say about you that matters. What you say about you is so much more powerful because not only do you say it, you hear it and you live it. Tell yourself every day that you're awesome and capable and there's no limit to your potential (more on self-motivation can be found in Chapter Nine: Next Steps).

FEAR OF RESPONSIBILITY

For some people, the scariest question they can ask themselves is, *What if I try something and fail?* For others, it's *What if I try and* succeed*?* Nothing can make you think, *I don't know if I'm capable of this* like comparing the life you've settled for to the life you really want and realizing all the work that it will require.

You have to be willing to look objectively at the commitment your dream will require and decide if that is something you're willing to undertake.

When I launched my law firm in 2018, I was worried about what all that responsibility meant for me. As the firm grew to 150 employees, the responsibilities grew as well, and I had two choices: I could shy away from the success, or I could embrace the responsibility. I opted for the latter, and every day, I've had to shoulder more responsibility than I ever have before.

I had to think critically about how becoming easily recognizable is going to affect various aspects of my life because everywhere I go now, people are going to know who I am. I can never go out looking like a bum. My car always has to be clean. My social media presence has to be strong. My house has to be well maintained. I have to embrace that responsibility because it is now part of becoming who I was meant to be.

SOWING YOUR SEEDS

If you have experienced any of the above and are yet to discover your own seeds of greatness, don't fret. You can start any time, no matter how much negativity you've had to overcome to this point. It took me a long time to figure out what I was created to do, and after so long, the lack of knowing or understanding what I was meant for in this life started to wear on me. I started becoming fearful that the best of me was not going to be shared with the people who needed it. By my freshman year of college, I was starting to feel depressed. I didn't have many friends. I'd been assigned two roommates, neither of whom I had ever met. At first, I thought they were cool but because I didn't drink or smoke, it soon became clear we did not have many shared values. I didn't feel like I fit in at all.

I was going to give up. I called my dad and told him I was going to come home, but he made short work of letting me know that was not an option. "Come home to what?" he asked. "There's nothing to come home to. You went there to play baseball. You're going to stay there. I know it's tough, but you have to see it through."

That night, I had what I call my "rooftop experience." I was living in a second-floor apartment and from my window, you could access the roof. I crawled up, looked at the night sky, and felt compelled to talk to God. "What is this life all about?" I asked. "This cannot be it. There has to be something better. Here I am down in the dumps, depressed, not feeling joy. You have to tell me something. Show me something. Do something. Give me a sign." I sat up there for hours, just watching the night sky and convincing myself that I had to quit, the sooner the better.

The very next day, God sent his sign. It came in the form of a new friend, a guy named Jesse. Jesse was on the baseball team, but I had never spoken a word to him because we'd only had a few practices by then. When we started talking, he invited me to go to his church to eat pizza on youth night. That one act showed me there was something more to college beyond the life I was living. Jesse ended up becoming my roommate, and the next two years set the trajectory for the rest of my life. I didn't quit. I ended up transferring to the University of West Georgia, then went on to become an attorney, then a partner, and now the owner of my own firm.

Allowing myself to be vulnerable opened me up to an opportunity I might never otherwise have considered. Had I not looked within enough to know I was not on the path I was intended to travel, I never would have been looking for a friend like Jesse who could help propel me in the direction I was meant to go. One of the reasons so many people struggle with becoming who they are is because the pain they have experienced in their lives has shattered their ability to be vulnerable. When you allow yourself to be vulnerable, people come into your life, and you are able to recognize the value in them and the impact they could have on you. Had I not been vulnerable, I might not have been as receptive to a friendship with Jesse, and had he offered the same invitation, I might have just said no. Talk about a missed opportunity or giving up too soon.

One of the reasons we allow haters, self-limiting beliefs, self-doubt, and quitting to keep us from our dreams is because we are not in touch with who we are and the source of our true power, because we've never wanted to become vulnerable. But how can you connect to the seed of greatness when you don't open yourself up to all the world has to offer you?

FINDING MY PURPOSE

After my rooftop experience, I was certain I was made for something more and I started searching for what that was. I was not going to be satisfied until I figured it out. I started by heeding my dad's advice and opening every single door of opportunity presented to me. I took on several jobs. I worked at American Eagle, at an exterminating job, at a sandwich shop, and cutting grass. I got more involved in school, taking a position as a mentor and translator and becoming president of the student athlete advisory committee. I did everything I could to participate in discovering who I was meant to be.

I was trying just about anything I could to help me understand what I was good at and what I was bad at, so when a local judge offered me a unique internship, I jumped on it. I worked one week each in eight different offices: magistrate court, state court, superior court, the district attorney's office, the solicitor's office, the police department, the sheriff's department, and with a defense attorney. I experienced all parts of the law and started getting a sense of what appealed to me most (more on this amazing period of my life and the importance of finding a mentor like the judge in Chapter Nine: Next Steps). Ultimately, I ended up taking a position as an interpreter for a law firm. I stayed at that firm for nearly fifteen years because I knew it was the place for me. I went on to become a legal assistant, then got into marketing, then started meeting clients, and by then, I knew I needed to be an attorney.

In law school, I realized I loved the business side of running a firm. I started reading more and more about the legal field but not about being a lawyer—I was learning how to run a law business. I consumed anything I could find related to management, operations, and leadership.

The opportunity to become a manager of the firm where I worked presented itself, and again, I jumped at it. I felt empowered, because by then not only did I know what I needed to do, but I knew why—I genuinely loved it. That experience eventually led me to where I am today, enjoying the success and fulfillment that comes with running my own firm and now helping other law firms do the exact same. It was a journey that lasted nearly fifteen years, but by the end of it, I had discovered what I was great at. If I would have quit during any period of that journey, I would not have succeeded at the level that I did.

KEEPING YOUR GREATNESS ALIVE

Despite discovering my purpose, I have not given myself permission to stay still. I'm always taking action to continue developing myself each and every day.

I still remain open to any opportunity that comes my way—

any conference, any networking event, any new person I can meet, any new book I can read. I always want to answer the door when there's a knock. In those moments, I feel I am living my best life because I'm never scared to embrace something new.

To find your own seeds of greatness, I encourage you to develop an intentional plan of self-discovery. I will delve deeper into this in Chapter Nine: Next Steps, but for now, I want you to start thinking about the ways you can dedicate time and energy to learning who you are. You might have to start committing yourself to things you've never previously considered. You may have a nine-to-five job, but during the evenings and weekends, you might have to start devoting time to other endeavors. You may need to find someone who is willing to hire you as a part-time real estate agent to see if you enjoy that. You may need to call up your friend who owns a restaurant and ask to shadow them for a day if that business interests you. You might need to volunteer at an animal rescue or join a book club or do anything at all related to any potential passion you're interested in exploring.

While you're doing this, you cannot be afraid to try anything, no matter how fruitless it initially may seem. I have a friend who traveled to Italy and came back with a newfound passion for pasta sauce. He developed his own recipe and to see if it was actually any good, he hosted a small dinner for friends. They liked it, so he decided to do another. And another. Eventually, he ended up quitting his job and devoting all his time to hosting these dinners and promoting his sauce. Today, complete strangers pay to attend his dining experiences. I went to one hosted in an Atlanta high-rise where fifteen people, none of whom knew each other, all had paid money to be there. His story is just one example of why I encourage everyone to simply start getting their feet wet in the field they're passionate about. (You can find his book *Gratitude and Pasta* by Chris Schembra on Amazon.)

As you begin to explore new avenues, remember the critical importance of having a strong support system of motivators and encouragers around you. You have to surround yourself with people who really want the best for you. And be selective, especially if you are the type of person who tends to assume everyone truly has your best interests in mind. Les Brown said, "The truth of the matter is that 20 percent of people don't care what you're going through. The other 80 percent are happy you're going through it." It can be tricky finding people who genuinely care about your journey, who want to be there in the struggle, and who want to see all your goals come to fruition. We live in a "me society" where everyone is so egocentric and so self-centered, it can be hard to find people who really care about you. But before you launch into any new endeavor, you have to develop a team of people who are going to encourage you along the way.

In order to achieve anything great, you have to have people around you who are going to motivate you and inspire you, and those are two different things. Motivation is what gets you excited; inspiration moves you to action. There are plenty of great motivators out there, but not all of them can inspire you into action. Every week, I hear different people speak and while some of them have great points, when I'm done listening, I'm not moved to do anything. Other times, I listen to motivational videos or read a book that takes me beyond motivation and makes me want to become something more. Find things that inspire your passion for life and success and find people who can inspire you this way.

You have to be intentional about finding a mentor. No matter what goal you're trying to accomplish—whether it be losing weight or starting a business or anything that's going to take any kind of risk—you first have to seek out somebody who's going to be your cheerleader. Think about the person in your life who can encourage you at all times, who can uplift you whenever you feel like you can't go any farther. Can they be your designated supporter? Or maybe there's a workout group you can join, a local business networking meeting you can attend. Think about the things you want in your life and find the people who are going to help you get them.

Can you think of anyone who has that effect on you? For me, it's always been my dad. I remember countless times in my life when something he said or did had a profound impact on my actions. One happened in college, when I transferred from a Division 1 school to a Division 2 school. Seeing that I was a starter on the baseball team at the D1 school, I assumed I'd start in my new home. But for whatever reason, I couldn't get any traction on the team, despite the fact that I played well. I wasn't starting, and it became a very frustrating time for me.

One day, between a doubleheader, I sulked up to my dad who had come to cheer on my team. He immediately saw the defeat in me.

"Do you smell that?" he said.

"What?" I asked, confused.

"Just take a second and breathe it in." He took a deep breath and exhaled. "Do you smell that?"

I did the same, brow furrowed. "It smells like the outside."

"It's the freshly cut grass," he said. "I want you to remember that smell, because one day you're not going to be able to play this game. One day you're not going to be able to compete. One day, you're not going to be able to be on this field and smell the grass and do the thing you love. Just remember that and enjoy it today."

In that moment, I realized I was spending so much time worrying about things that didn't matter and letting them create negativity in my life. I needed that inspiration, that person who was capable of helping me see the bigger picture and focus on the present. And man was he right. Today I wish more than anything that I could go back to that moment and play just one more time.

To activate your own greatness, you need your own people who inspire you. Otherwise, you will exist alone on an island with no one to strengthen your spirit when you need it most. And you cannot do it alone. Nobody has achieved anything of great significance without a team of supporters behind them.

OVER-ENCOURAGEMENT IS IMPOSSIBLE

I always say my dad is the "I told you so" person, but in the best possible way. If I tell him, "We just hit a huge milestone in our business," his response is always, "I told you that was going to happen." He's been such an encourager my whole life, constantly telling me, "You're going to do great. You're going to succeed. You're going to go to college and play baseball. You're going to become a lawyer. Your business is going to grow. You're going to be popular on the speaking circuit. Everybody is going to want to read your book."

Nowadays, people are critical of such attitudes. They say over-encouragement is harmful because when people are always told they can do everything they want to, they don't know how to fail. People are particularly critical of this trait in parents of millennials. There's a common perception that because those parents told their kids they were capable of anything, today's young adults expect everything to be handed to them. I believe there's a huge difference between spoiling your child and encouraging your child, and personally, I don't think anyone can overdo the latter. Using my dad as my example, I find every opportunity to let my own children know I believe in them.

I ran a 5K with my two boys, ages six and nine. Halfway through, my oldest, Ruly, turned to me and said, "Daddy, I can't do it." He said he was thirsty and tired. He wanted to quit. I stopped him right there and said, "I don't ever want to hear you say again, 'I can't do this.' You can do this. We'll get you water. You'll be fine and you will finish this race."

"But I can't," he said.

"Ruly," I said, "you absolutely can. We're going to finish together. You can do this." We crossed that finish line together in thirty-eight minutes. We were so happy. But most importantly, Ruly will look back on that day and know even when he doubted himself, I never did and for the rest of his life, I never will.

NO REGRETS

By now I hope you understand how your life cannot be experienced the way it's intended to be experienced until you embrace who you are intended to be. The depth of your existence here on earth is enhanced by finding who you were created to be. Only once you do that can you fully activate the greatness within you. Your greatness is what unlocks your passion, and your passion unlocks your possibilities.

If fear is keeping you from taking that step, you have to recognize that fear is nowhere near as powerful as the regret you'll feel by living a life you were not intended to live. You only have one life to live—why not make it the best life possible? Why live in fear when you can live in victory? Why live in defeat when you can live in triumph? You have to find the thing that gets you up every morning and then pursue it with a relentless passion. When you do, you will achieve greater things than you could have ever imagined, and you will be happier than you could have ever thought possible.

Even if you have regrets about the way you've lived your life so far, you can learn from those feelings and experiences and use them to help propel you away from the life you don't want and toward achieving the goals most important to you today. Pull out the positive and view the rest as a stop on your journey toward the quest you're meant for. It might have been a detour, but you're still on the road to all you are supposed to achieve.

If you let the fear win and allow it to keep you from chasing your real dreams, you're going to live a life of unhappiness. You're going to be perpetually unsatisfied with the circumstances of your life and eventually, you're going to start to blame others because unhappiness tends to look out instead of in. To avoid examining your own failures and faults, you'll point fingers and risk ending up bitter and isolated. You will begin to believe you are not created to be great and you will look at your life with regret, believing nothing can be changed. You will end up wasting your life and depriving the world of the greatness you have within you.

CHAPTER FOUR EXERCISE

To tap into your own greatness, write down ten courageous decisions you'd have to make to live the life you want. For each, ask yourself, *Am I willing to be courageous and do this?* Your answers will help you identify the things holding you back and determine if you are truly ready for the success you say you want. Next ask, *What steps do I need to take today to move into the direction of that courageous decision?*

CHAPTER FIVE

BOUNCING BACK

HOW TO GROW FROM FAILURE

"Failure is simply the opportunity to begin again, this time more intelligently."

—HENRY FORD

Chances are, you may already have tried to chase one of your dreams. Maybe you started a business, launched a career, opened a restaurant or store, and the reason you're reading this book right now is because whatever you did failed and now you have no idea what to do with yourself. Your self-doubt is off the charts, you're questioning every decision you make, and you're stuck, terrified to take a step in any direction.

I have been there many, *many* times. Over the course of my life, I have launched multiple businesses, and each and every one tanked. I know what it feels like to think everything you touch is going to fail. But I've also learned that professional failure is not always as bad as we make it out to be for two reasons:

1. Failure doesn't define you—what you do after you fail does.
2. You are so much more than your professional identity.

I know now that no one thing can ever be solely responsible for my self-worth. But it took many trials and tribulations for me to understand that lesson and many others as I grew into the businessman I am today.

EARLY ENTREPRENEURSHIP

For as long as I can remember, I've always tried to figure out ways to make money. It's a trait I already can tell I'm passing down to my son. He's ten and *always* asking how he can earn money. He'll ask, "Daddy, what chores will you pay me to do?" It makes me smile because he actually wants to sweep, take out the trash, and clean the bathroom. He also has an unlimited supply of back rubs and head scratches, all for the low price of one dollar apiece, and that's exactly how I was when I was little.

My first experience with working was in the food delivery business. Long before there was Uber Eats, there was Luis Eats, and I had exactly one client. I was the guy who went and picked up milk and bread for my grandmother from the local store. In return, she would pay me the difference of the amount she gave me and the amount I spent. So, if she gave me $3 to get milk and eggs and the bill was $2.25, I got to keep the 75 cents. It was my very first hustle. I was loaded!

My next gig was helping carry cement for a construction crew working on an addition at my grandmother's home that same summer. Between the two gigs, I pulled in $33 in three months. It was the best summer of my life from a financial standpoint.

By high school, I had moved up in the world and took on

a whole new role as housekeeper for my parents. In my new position, I had four basic responsibilities: cut the grass front and back, wash both cars inside and out, clean both bathrooms, and iron all my parents' clothes. Mind you, I have three siblings, but none of them was ever out in the yard with the push mower. None of them was vacuuming inside my parents' cars. None of them was scrubbing the bathrooms or even going anywhere near the iron.

Every week, this list of chores took up my weekends. And by the end of it all, I had earned $20 (allow me to remind you this was not the 1950s—it was 1998. Twenty bucks barely covered the cost of a new CD). But to me, it didn't matter. I knew if I needed something, my parents would always find a way to get it for me because I worked so hard. When I went to prom, they found a way to get a gift for my date. When I had birthdays or I needed to travel to go to a game, they always found a way to help me. And so, my initial experiences with entrepreneurship only fueled my hunger to go out and make something of myself on my own. I just wasn't yet sure how I was going to do that.

A TOUGH PILL TO SWALLOW

In my senior year of college, I had my first opportunity to give real-life entrepreneurship a try. I started selling vitamins through a multilevel marketing company. Today, such companies are common. Think It Works! or Herbalife. People market them all over social media today, but back in 2004, that wasn't common practice. We didn't have Facebook—heck, we didn't even have the first iPhone yet. I started off really hot. In my first three months, I was making $1,000 a month. But as a twenty-year-old, I lacked something I critically needed to sustain such success: the emotional stability to manage the ups and downs of business ownership. I had recruited forty-five people to sell the product and had no idea how to effectively deal with them.

I kept going for four years, but ultimately, I failed because I simply wasn't capable of managing people and keeping it together. I spent a lot of time being scared of what people were going to say and in sales, people turn you down a lot. I couldn't handle it, and the negativity I felt began to shape my thought process and ability to lead as a business owner. However, there is an upside. I didn't know it at the time, but that experience (and several others like it) was developing me into the business owner I am today. It taught me that people are going to be negative, but you will live. Some people are going to say no, but you're still going to sell to others.

The question is: Are you going to push through it? Are you going to keep moving forward even when it seems as if nobody's in your corner? Even though that company failed, the experience taught me you have to push through and keep working no matter what happens.

FAILURE DOESN'T DEFINE YOU—WHAT YOU DO AFTER YOU FAIL DOES.

DROPPING OUT OF THE RACE

My next moneymaking attempt came just as the 2008 presidential election was heating up. Barack Obama was inspiring more young people to get engaged in politics, and I decided my friend and I would write a political blog. I had heard *The Huffington Post* started as a blog and was now bringing in $500 million in revenue. It seemed so easy. All we had to do was write posts and people would read them—piece of cake. I talked a few of my friends into working for me, recruited a few younger, politically minded people, and ended up with a roster of fifteen. We prepared our first posts, promoted the site like crazy, hosted a "grand opening" dinner, and on the first day the site was live, we got a whopping sixty views. One of my Facebook posts gets more than that today. But I insisted on pushing forward, figuring the content would attract more people soon enough. Turned out, content was my next big problem.

On our first day, we had eighteen new articles. By day five, we had four. Less than a week in, well over half my staff had quit because they couldn't take the negative feedback from some readers (we were up to about five hundred page views total by that point), and I had no one to write for the site. And they also didn't have the passion for it. Truth was neither did I. I was just trying to make a quick buck.

Within three weeks, the staff was down to me, and I was only able to produce one blog post a day. No content meant no views, which meant no ads and therefore, no money. By week four, the site was down.

I didn't know anything about blogging back then. I had no idea the time it took to build an audience and a reliable list of contributors. I had no clue that some of the blogs that launched at the exact same time mine did would still be going strong ten years later because they saw the site as a long-term investment rather than a make-money-quick idea. The people behind those sites planned to stay committed for the long haul from the onset, and now they're making millions.

My failure was in my willingness to accept defeat before the site even had a chance to grow. If I would've just stayed steady and just kept blogging once a day, every day, I could have possibly created something lasting.

SWING AND A MISS

By this point, I was working at the law firm, but that didn't stop me from looking for another million-dollar idea. I decided my next move would be with…another vitamin company! I can just see you rolling your eyes but in my defense, this one seemed like a knockout punch from the get-go.

It all started when a friend told me he had landed a meeting with a legendary boxer from Atlanta and wanted me there as his legal representation. The plan was to pitch a partnership with a company that made vitamins that reduced joint inflammation and made living with arthritis easier. The boxer already swore by the product, so we were hoping to connect him to the Arthritis Foundation and launch a global campaign.

We were invited to the boxer's mansion. I pulled up to the security gate in front of the biggest house I've ever been to in my life, fully expecting to be turned away. But my name was on the list, they let me in, and I proceeded to gape at the over-the-top luxury. The garage had three limousines. He had a bowling alley in his home. The dining-room table sat twenty-eight. The pool belonged at a five-star resort—he told me the water bill just to fill it was $25,000.

As we got to know him more while exploring our proposed partnership, the exciting experiences kept coming. I got to see a fight in Las Vegas. I got to attend several NASCAR events sponsored by the Arthritis Foundation and the vitamin company and meet some of the top-name drivers. But as all this was going on, my friend and I came to realize the funding promised to us from a few different sources wasn't coming through.

We had talked to multiple people about raising money and had gotten plenty of positive responses. Multiple sources had promised us millions, but those promises always went unfulfilled for one reason or another. It took me a while to understand they all were only saying they would help us out because it meant a chance to meet the celebrity boxer. They never had any intention of giving us any money. They were trying to raise their personal stock by meeting him to see if they could use him for something.

This time, the business failed because I didn't realize the importance of doing actual work, like securing funding. We never made a penny out of the deal.

BAD BID

Now, I was going to law school, but I didn't know exactly where that was going to take me. Again, I needed to figure out a way to make more money, and this time, I decided to start an auction website.

I created a site where people could bid on an item a penny at a time over and over until the last person dropped out. Then, whoever had the highest bid was the "winner" who got to buy the item. So, if someone won an iPad for $13.88, that meant there were 1,388 bids.

By now, I had learned about the importance of startup capital, and I convinced a friend to split the $20,000 cost to launch the site with me. We bought $20,000 worth of prizes and set up the site. Within a week, we had generated $7,000 in revenue— but we were also out of prizes. We took that $7,000, reinvested it, had less prizes the following week, and the negative reviews started pouring in. Everyone was saying the website was no good because after a week, we were offering half the prizes we'd started with.

Despite the flak, we ended up generating $10,000 in revenue the next week. But realizing how unlikely it was that we could sustain the site, we both decided to bail. And because I had dragged him in, I gave my friend the full $10,000 and took the loss myself.

This time, I had wildly underestimated the amount of work the site was going to take. For instance, if we had $5,000 worth of $20 gift cards, that was 250 gift cards we had to mail. We didn't have professionally produced envelopes—I was mailing them myself in envelopes I bought at Walmart. I realized I had to be much more calculated in making decisions. I'm a firm believer in going after the things you want, but you have to think about everything it's going to require of you before you do.

If I were to start the same business now (which I wouldn't) I would start by creating an appealing site, then making sure I had letterhead and a professional mailing system in place. I'd also make sure I got people to join the site to establish a following before I put $20,000 worth of prizes on it, rather than having the same handful of people winning everything again and again.

I learned you have to be thoughtful and calculated. You have to have as much information as you can and establish a clear and dedicated path to resolving whatever issues might lie ahead.

STRIKEOUT

All my life, the one thing I was sure I knew inside and out was baseball. Even though I had graduated law school by this point, anytime anyone would ask me, "What would you do if you could do anything at all?" I still always said, "I would be a baseball coach." With that in mind, I launched my next venture: a baseball recruiting business.

Travel ball is really big around the country, and a lot of people spend thousands of dollars for their kids to play in the leagues. A former Minor League player who knew my baseball background pitched me an idea, and I liked it right away. Our plan was to use our connections to find coaches from different cities and set up teams all over the country.

We designed a logo, made shirts for the players and ourselves and set out trying to recruit players. We quickly learned it was not going to be as easy as we'd assumed because although the kids were impressed by our baseball backgrounds, the parents really didn't care who we were. All they cared about was sending their kids to the best, most established program. No one wanted to be the first to sign up with us, and after a few weeks, we'd only managed to recruit one kid.

I started to question this idea's viability, but my partner insisted we keep at it. He encouraged me to work harder, visit schools, show up at practices, set up meetings with parents. But I was a practicing lawyer at the time, and there was no way I had the time for all of that. I told him I'd gladly continue reaching out to people I knew, but I couldn't commit to making this a full-time job. He got upset and said if my heart wasn't really in it, I should just give him my T-shirt back and bow out. Which I gladly did.

This time, I learned that going into business with someone you don't really know is a stupid thing to do. In this case, I just loved baseball and wanted to share that with kids. He wanted to make this the main focus of his life. We were never on the same page. When you work with a partner, you have to be equally committed and aligned. If you don't share the same fire and drive, you'll both fail.

THE MOTHER OF ALL FAILURES

You might find it hard to believe that after all of that, I still hadn't experienced what I consider the most significant failure of my professional life. From the outside looking in, it might seem relatively minor compared to what I'd already gone through.

But to me, the dissolution of my partnership at the law firm where I'd spent nearly fifteen years changed the trajectory of my life in ways I never could have anticipated, and for that, it is my Mother of All Failures.

I spent some time in Chapter Three detailing the course of my career at the firm, but as a quick recap, I'll remind you I had started there at age twenty-two as a Spanish interpreter, one of three total employees. I worked there while I finished my undergraduate degree in accounting and decided to stay simply because I liked it. I had offers from two other companies—a construction business and an accounting firm—for a lot more money, but I stuck it out with my $15-an-hour salary at the firm because I was starting to realize I really wanted to become a lawyer.

By the summer of 2005, I was a full-time legal assistant and they let me try my hand at bringing in some business. As it turned out, a I had a natural knack for that aspect of the business, and after a month, we had tripled our new client list from ten to thirty a month.

By the time I graduated law school, the firm was up to twenty-four employees, and I knew if I was going to stay, I needed some serious incentive. I prepared a 125-page binder making a case for why they should consider making me partner. I was bringing in 80 percent of the business, I had been working my butt off, and I wanted my worth at the firm to be rewarded appropriately. They resisted at first, but after several rounds of negotiations, we agreed I would stay on for another two years as an attorney before they made me partner.

I walked out of the meeting and called my dad, excited to share my news. "Be careful," he said. "Be careful about what?" I asked, caught off guard by his response. "Don't ever forget," he said, "they don't *want* you to be a partner."

At the time, it seemed like a strange thing for a parent to

tell his son who just announced he was going to be a partner of a law firm. But Dad saw immediately something it took me several more years to understand: the importance of alignment.

In retrospect, I don't know how I missed the writing on the wall. For the four years I was partners with these people, I never once had dinner with any of them. I was never invited to any of their homes. Our priorities never aligned: I wanted to spend money on marketing, and they didn't. I wanted to spend money on networking events, consulting, learning, and growing, and they didn't. It was a totally misaligned, disconnected relationship, and when it ended, it should have come as no surprise to me. But it did, and in one unceremonious meeting, the course of my life was forever altered.

My failure was not fully understanding that partnership requires joint desire and mutual alignment. As soon as I'd graduated law school, I received five offers for employment without even applying. Other firms wanted me to come work for them because they knew how much business I could generate, and they knew about the connections that I had cultivated. I turned them all down because the firm I had a history with finally gave me a partnership.

Perhaps my biggest mistake was relying on past success to prove my worth. I kept pointing to what I had already done for the firm to make my case for being partner when I should have been focusing on what I could do in the future and making sure that was in alignment with what the other partners wanted. Today, I never take any achievement for granted. My current firm is enjoying great success, but I continue to treat it as if we haven't done anything. I don't ever want to lose sight like I did last time, and I certainly never want to find myself in a similar position ever again. I keep working as if it's my first day on the job, which is the opposite of what I did the first time around.

But the real reason the collapse of the partnership is the mother of all failures is because I had dedicated nearly fifteen years of my life to something that was not my true calling. That firm was never going to be an environment where I could let my real talents shine. Instead of taking a step back and realizing that earlier on, I stayed on because I felt like I was obligated to them for how good they had been to me over the years.

This had nothing to do with them and everything to do with me. It was my ambition, my naivete and my misalignment that caused this failure. To this day, I credit them largely for my success because of all that I learned in those fifteen years. But this failure hurt me deeply. My entire identity was this firm. That's what everyone knew me for and now I was losing that.

MY BIGGEST MISTAKE WAS RELYING ON PAST SUCCESS TO PROVE MY WORTH.

YOU ARE MORE THAN YOUR JOB

The longer you're in a situation that is not representative of who you were called to be, the easier it is to believe there's no hope for you. When I look back at my time at the law firm, I remember friends, colleagues, business associates, even my pastor, telling me, "You need to get out of that partnership." Everyone could see I was not happy and my value was unappreciated. I would respond, saying, "But they've been so good to me. They helped me pay for law school. I've been here fifteen years—I can't just leave them now."

In saying and believing such things, I began to lose my own identity as an entrepreneur. I started convincing myself all my businesses had failed because of my own shortcomings, and therefore it made no sense to ever take the plunge again. I needed to stay because I could not make it on my own. Staying in that job kept me from activating my seeds of greatness and becoming the person I needed to be because I was letting my job define me. It didn't occur to me that the thing I was allowing to take over my identity was not something worthy of my time and attention.

There is great danger in letting what you do professionally define who you are as a person. When you can only find your self-worth and value as an individual within the work you do, you risk losing who you are completely should you ever not be able to do that job. In my profession representing injured workers, I've met many people whose professions are their key identifying factors. Mechanics, professional athletes, radio personalities, nurses—anyone and everyone is capable of letting their line of work determine who they are and how they see themselves.

What does it even mean to find your self-worth in what you do? Aren't who you are and what you do the same thing? There are some cases when this actually is true. If you're a pastor, for instance, you are a religious figure. That line of work does define who you are. But for most of us, what we do is just a small part of who we are. I am a lawyer, but that's not all of who I am. I'm also:

- A father
- A husband
- A friend
- A son
- A brother
- A business owner
- An entrepreneur
- A visionary
- A risk-taker
- An encourager

Being a lawyer is just a small part of who I am, and my role as a lawyer should be defined by who I am, not the other way around.

When we define who we are by what we do but then lose the ability to do that job, we can find ourselves in despair. This happens often with injured professional athletes who can no longer perform, singers who can no longer sing, actors who can no longer act. They find themselves in a desperate situation, because in their minds, all of who they were was that persona. It is harmful to place so much emphasis, stress, and pressure on the work we do, because it can be taken away from us at any moment for any number of reasons.

For me, the experience of losing the ability to perform as a baseball player was eye-opening. I had to figure out another way to define myself, and that sent me on a long journey of self-discovery. If I wasn't a baseball player, who was I? It took time, but I eventually realized I'm a charitable guy. I'm a kind person. I'm a professional. I'm smart. I'm accommodating. I'm responsible. Those qualities make up who I am. They are the characteristics that define me. Once I was able to identify them, I discovered that no matter what I decided to do professionally, I'd be able to do it with a tremendous sense of joy.

But again, it took time to get there. For the first ten years of my fifteen-year ride at the firm, my self-worth was rooted in the fact that I could generate business and bring in clients. When I transitioned into a role not directly tied to the generation of new revenue, I found myself asking the question, "Am I worthy?" It felt like if I didn't bring in clients, I had no value to my partners. In their minds, if I didn't bring in clients, I wasn't doing anything, despite the fact that I was managing the firm.

Separating myself from bringing in clients required a mental shift when it came to thinking about my value. I had to ask myself, *What am I actually contributing to the firm?* My value was in managing the firm, the people, the systems, and the operations. That was who I was. I had thought I was a rainmaker, but when I stepped back and really thought about it, I realized that wasn't the case. I'm actually a great businessperson—I just happen to also be good at generating revenue.

The eventual dissolution of the partnership confirmed my suspicions that my partners saw me as a great rainmaker but a lousy businessman. They didn't think I made good business decisions. Despite the fact that we had reorganized the business, adopted new policies and procedures, introduced a new software program, and generally done a lot of things right, because I was not generating the business I used to, I had no worth. It started taking an emotional toll on me.

I spent two weeks sulking and basically not doing anything other than trying to regroup.

A month after the dissolution, I started my own law practice, and within just a few months, I had over one hundred new clients and a new opportunity knocking at the door, which became the partnership I'm in today. My current partner saw who I actually was. He understood I was not a rainmaker. He saw that I am a great businessperson. He saw that I have integrity, am trustworthy, and strive for excellence. His ability to truly see me helped greatly in my recovery after one of the more painful moments in my life. He saw my value, and it made the dissolution much easier to swallow.

Today, I don't define myself by my work. I love to work—most days, I'm at the office at 8:00 a.m. and don't leave until 6:00 p.m. But if there's a day when I can't show up until 9:30 a.m., that's okay. I enjoy what I do, but I know my sense of self-worth is not found in it. It's a much more freeing way to live, because now, nobody can tell me who I am. Regardless of what others might think of me, I know who I am, and nothing they say can change that. I've already established that I'm a great businessman, father, husband, son, cousin, neighbor, and friend. That's who I am, and if someone doesn't think I'm good for one business, I know there's another out there that needs my help, and I can move on. I'm not going to be defined by this job. When you're not consumed by what you do, you know you can go anywhere and still be you.

FINDING SUCCESS THROUGH FAILURE

After the initial hurt of the end of the partnership wore off, I was able to see it for the blessing it actually was. Today, my life is completely different. Every morning, I wake up more inspired. During my last few years with the old firm, I remember not even wanting to wake up. I was tired all the time and depressed. If I had to be at work at 9:00 a.m., I would get up at 8:30 a.m. Sometimes, I wouldn't even shave. Then I'd work for a bit, come home for a two-and-a-half-hour lunch, put in a few more hours, and leave for the day by 4:30 p.m. I couldn't bear to be there any longer than that. Now, I'm up every day at 5:00 a.m. My renewed passion has completely changed my entire way of looking at life, and even my body has responded.

I am reading every single day. I go to the gym. I have full work–life integration. I now consult over seventy law firms on how to grow their businesses, and many of them are growing 50 percent or more every single year. And my seed of greatness, the me God wants me to be, is in the process of being shown to the entire world.

Finally activating your seed of greatness changes how you feel about yourself. It changes how you operate. It changes how you think. It changes how you work. It changes how you handle your finances. It changes how you conduct yourself in relationships. Today, I have stronger relationships than I've ever had before. I have deeper ties to the community. I never dread going to work, and it's all a result of doing what I'm called to do, which is managing and operating a business.

I can even look at all of my previous failures with a whole new perspective. I know now my skill set is not in starting a business. My skill set is in taking an established business and making it great. I wanted to do that at my old firm, but they didn't share my vision. So, I took that vision, applied it to my own firm, and now we'll represent about six thousand clients this year. I went from managing a firm of twenty-four employees with no vision to managing a firm of more than 150, all inspired by a shared vision.

Tapping into my true passion also impacted my personal life. It inspired me to start reading again, which I believe is key to growing as a person. I personally believe bettering myself through reading led to me tripling my income in one year (much more on this in Chapter Nine: Next Steps). I'm happily married. I'm living in a new city. I have season tickets to the Braves, Atlanta United, and the Hawks. I travel seven to ten weeks per year. I enjoy life more than ever, and it's all because I was finally able to become the person I was truly meant to be.

LOOKING FORWARD

If you have yet to start living a life you find equally fulfilling, I encourage you to ask yourself the question: what can I see myself doing for the rest of my life? Because activating your seed of greatness is not a temporary act—it will change you forever. I always find it funny when people say, "I can't wait to retire, then I'll be able to do all the things I want to do." If you're living your true calling, it should be the thing you always want to do. Why would you want to retire from the thing you were created to do? You don't retire from life.

If you feel yourself being pulled to a profession you don't know much about, I encourage you to gain some experience before diving in. I've always believed my wife Rachel was meant to be an entrepreneur. For years, she has resisted the urge, claiming she just wants to have a job and a steady income. But now that she's married to someone who owns a business, she's starting to realize there's tremendous freedom and power in doing what you love. Now, she's starting to consider opening a gym. It makes perfect sense: she loves working out, she's in great shape, and she loves wearing athleisure wear. But she's never worked in a gym. So rather than quitting her job and jumping into something she's never tried before, I suggested she get her personal training certificate first. Then she can train a couple clients to make sure she really enjoys doing the work. It's okay to start with small steps toward your dream if you're not in a position to totally upend your life.

You must look at your dream as at least a ten-year investment. Unless you die, you will be ten years older in ten years. And you will either have achieved your dreams or allowed fear and disappointment to hold you back.

I'd also caution you to stop expecting a bigger paycheck, an upgraded office, the next promotion, or anything else of the sort to make you genuinely happy. I once heard a prominent speaker ask an audience of people how much money was enough money. People started yelling out all kinds of figures: $75,000! $1 million! "No, no, no, no," the speaker said. "Enough money is just a little bit more than what you make right now." The point was that no matter how much we make, we always have the tendency to think, *If I just made a little bit more, then*

I would be happy. If I could just drive the Range Rover instead of the RAV4. But the person who's driving the Range Rover is thinking, *If I could just drive the G-Wagon, then I'd be happy.* The person who's driving the G-Wagon is thinking, *If I could just drive the Cullinan...* We never let ourselves be satisfied with what we have, and it can cloud our ability to recognize the things that truly matter.

As a business owner, I see this all the time. Some people work for us for less than a year then put in a resignation because they got another job that's going to pay them $1,000 more a year. That's $80 a month. They will actually quit their job and uproot themselves for the cost of one nice dinner a month. But they can't resist the "bigger" number on their paycheck. Nine times out of ten, once they get into that new job, they have regrets but are too prideful to come back. The bottom line is you cannot spend your life expecting a job to make you happy—you have to *be* happy, then you will enjoy the job you have.

There are people who are always looking for a better environment, a better relationship, a better job, thinking it's going to be perfect. They assume this new situation will magically erase any unhappiness or hardship they're experiencing. But the only way to guarantee the future time is better than the past time is what you do in the meantime, and many people don't do anything in the meantime. They assume the future is going to be better than the past, but they don't do anything while they're waiting for their future. They don't change or grow. They go nowhere because they're not bettering themselves. Many times, they don't realize they need to grow. But that's not you because you are reading this book. You know growth is necessary for success.

When I worked at my old law firm, while I was training, growing, developing, and reading, everyone was laughing at me. I came to work every day in a full suit while everyone else wore button-downs and slacks. These are the same people who were making $50,000 a year when I started there fifteen years ago and are making $60,000 a year today. I, on the other hand, went from making $12 an hour then to $1,000 an hour today because I made sure what I did in the "meantime" mattered.

The key is to realize your journey toward self-improvement is a process. It's not going to be easy, and you'll have to work through a lot of things, but those are just stepping stones to achieving the things you want. And people will ridicule you and put you down. They will tell lies about you and spread rumors and gossip. You just have to take a step every single day toward your goal.

AVOIDING BURNOUT

While finding work you love is important, you must also avoid letting your whole life circle around your job, because when you do, you risk burning out and losing the drive that initially made you interested in the career to begin with. Your professional life should be just one part of your life, not all of your life.

The true reason people burn out is not because they have too much work or they work too long or too hard; they burn out because they don't grow. Just like in the weight room, the stronger you get, the longer you can last. I felt that way at the old firm because I was letting the job define me. I thought, *If I just work hard enough, people are going to think that I am great.* Today, I let the talents and strengths I possess define my job, not the other way around. If you're impressed by what I do or not, it doesn't matter to me, because that's not who I am. I know I'm doing a great job, and I'm going to continue to do a great job, enjoy what I do, and be happy. My passion is fueled by simply knowing who I am. When you're happy and comfortable with who you are, you can never burn out. And also, it becomes harder to be swayed by the opinions of other people.

Similarly, one of the reasons people go from job to job, business to business, relationship to relationship is because they're seeking passion. When someone says, "I don't love you like I used to," what they're really saying is, "I don't feel the passion I used to feel when we first met." But true passion does not come from "newness"—true passion is everlasting. In a relationship, passion is driven by the desire to really want to develop a commitment with the other person. The same concept applies to your job. If you don't feel a drive to commit to something long term, you lack passion.

I once read that passion can be anything that simultaneously challenges you, intrigues you, and motivates you. Contrary to the idea that doing what you love makes work effortless, passion puts you to work. It's what you are willing to sacrifice lesser leisure and pleasures for.

WHY FAILURE IS A GOOD THING

Failure is an opportunity to learn what you did wrong and to learn how you're going to do it right in the future. When we fail, what we've really found is a way that doesn't work and gives us the opportunity to find a new way to do things better.

When my partnership ended, I filled an entire journal with ideas for a book I planned to call *Partnerships Suck*. In it, I explore ten pitfalls to partnerships, things you should avoid to make sure your partnership doesn't fail. When I wrote it, I had no idea six months later, I would be in a conversation with one of my best friends about becoming partners. But before we did, I read him the ten things I wrote about. We talked about our vision, mission, and core values; the expected work ethic; our desire to grow, to win, to be the best, to work with urgency; our ideas for the future; and expected alignment. And now I use this same book to consult other law firm owners who want to entertain partnership.

Failure taught me to look for all of these things in my next partnership. It allowed me to do it right the second time in a smarter way with more openness and transparency. For me, that failure was a huge success. Granted, it didn't feel great at the time, but it felt amazing at the end.

When you learn to actually enjoy the journey of your life and your path toward self-improvement, you can view failure as just another step toward success. The ability to see past any hardship you're experiencing to the end result of eventual joy will allow you to find opportunities to learn from all the mistakes you inevitably will make.

CHAPTER FIVE EXERCISES

To understand how your feelings on failure can impact you, ask yourself the following questions:

- When you think about failing, are you motivated or de-motivated to act?
- What are three things you want to be known for one year from now?
- What do you want to be defined by in five years?
- What do you want people to say about you when you die?

Then, ask yourself: have you let professional setbacks and past disappointment keep you from becoming those things?

CHAPTER SIX

THIS IS YOUR LIFE

HOW TO START LIVING THE WAY YOU WANT

"Don't be pushed around by the fears in your mind. Be led by the dreams in your heart."

—ROY T. BENNETT

I was thirty-four years old when I realized I needed to take my life into my own hands. The reason it took so long is because for my entire existence up until then, I had suffered from a debilitating fear of judgment from others: people I knew, people I didn't know, people I loved, people who were acquaintances, people I worked with, people I went to church with, *everyone*. I feared what they thought and what they might say about me so much that I was living a life that was not really reflective of who I wanted to be.

The old saying "hurting people hurt other people" started to apply directly to my life. Because I didn't know who I was, I could never truly dedicate myself to someone else. The destructive consequences of the state I was operating in became most evident when I made a life-changing commitment I was in no position to make.

A DOOMED UNION

A disclaimer before I share the story of my failed marriage: although I went through a divorce, I do not intend in any way to encourage you to do the same or lead you to believe divorce is the only way to be happy just because it has worked out for me. Divorce is a decision with serious consequences that can result in hurt for many people and should only be considered after deep personal reflection and receiving the advice of wise counsel. My divorce was fueled by the depression I didn't realize I had and much of what I perceived in my marriage was viewed through a flawed lens.

I met my ex when I was nineteen, and although we couldn't see it at the time, we had an uphill battle from the onset. The majority of our relationship was long-distance because I was away at college. During the entire time we were "dating" (in quotes because it's hard to date somebody who you live so far away from and who you barely see), my focus always lay elsewhere. For a period, my top priority was my pursuit of becoming a professional athlete. Later, I lasered in on becoming financially successful because by then, I was letting my job define me. Then I went to law school while working full time, never giving the relationship the investment it required. I was never happy with who I was or what I was doing, and therefore, it was almost impossible for me to be happy in a relationship.

Regardless, my ex and I remained a couple, and by four years in, she was fully embedded in my life and quite close with my family and friends. I assumed the expectation among everyone was for us to get married, and though I had suspicions something was not quite right, I felt I was in a position where I couldn't say no. I had orchestrated everything so there was no way I could take my own life into my own hands. I was living a life for people other than myself—primarily my family—because I was terrified of disappointing them and going against the life they saw for me. I didn't know how to say no or move in another direction. I was scared of disappointing people. I was scared of disappointing myself. I was just plain scared of everything.

The problem was, because of the long distance, I simply didn't really know my ex. But I had created a story in my mind in which my family would be so angry with me for going against their wishes, I had no choice but to marry her. I was certain they'd tell me I had to listen to them because they knew best and they wouldn't want me to make a mistake. It was all a construct of fear in my mind. None of it was true.

Nevertheless, we married and stayed together for ten years, during which we had two beautiful children. For that reason, I will never regret the relationship. But by a decade in, I was certain the marriage could not last any longer. I was depressed, immersed in despair, and the weight was becoming too much to bear. Because I was so good at the blame game at the time, I believed my marriage was the reason I couldn't get over my sadness. I made the drastic and dramatic decision to announce my desire for a divorce, catching my ex and almost every person who knew me completely off guard and sending shock waves through all of our friends and family.

It didn't make sense to anyone because my relationship with my then-wife actually was good. We did not argue. We got along great. We had similar religious beliefs. We parented together well. All signs pointed to a successful marriage. The only problem was that I was totally unhappy and I did not want to be married, which was an incredibly hurtful thing to tell someone. But I was certain ending the marriage was going to make me instantly happy. It didn't.

From the moment I made the decision to end my marriage,

everything about how I saw and lived my life changed. When everyone naturally demanded an explanation for my seemingly out-of-the-blue announcement, I told my parents about the immense pressure I had felt because of what I assumed they wanted for me. They were completely floored. They could not understand why on God's green earth I would have thought any of that. Because the truth is: they had *never done anything* to make me feel obligated to marry my ex. I had created that pressure in my mind all on my own. Everything I thought about how they saw me and my life was rooted in assumptions, and I let those assumptions determine my actions, resulting in inevitable pain and devastation for many people.

In reality, I was just too scared to say no, and I had created the perfect excuse in my mind to avoid it. There was no way I could speak up and say what I really wanted because it would hurt too many people—or at least that's what I told myself. In the end, I learned the pain of saying no today is always going to be less than the pain of hurting someone in the future.

Today, I live with the regret of bringing pain to someone who I could have avoided hurting had I just been strong enough to say no from the very beginning or had I been strong enough to get the support I needed for the unhappiness I felt. After four years of dating, I had been afraid my ex would feel like I had wasted her life if I didn't marry her. But instead of doing the brave thing and ending it then, I wasted even more of her life by staying in a relationship. Had I just had the courage to break up with her then, our families and friends would have gotten over it. We both likely would have met other people, fallen in love, and gotten married. Everything would have been fine.

In the long run, everything worked out for me and my ex as well, but the first year afterward was incredibly hard as we navigated the child support legal battle. Today, we have a cordial relationship and are both remarried and happy. But I still realize the pain I brought upon all involved—including myself—likely was intensified by my inability to take control of my own life. At the time, I was scared of the ridicule I'd face for breaking up with her. I ended up facing far more intense judgment for abruptly ending a marriage. Back then, I was scared of upsetting my friends. When my marriage ended, so did many of my friendships. The worst part of it all is that everything I was scared of ended up coming true tenfold.

RESIDUAL EFFECTS

When I left my marriage, the criticism came fast and from every source imaginable. People who barely knew me said I was abandoning my family. They assumed I was acting on impulse. They had no idea how many mornings I had sat in the shower and cried about the looming desperation and depression I carried around with me all day. They thought I was totally emotionless when it came to the relationship. I was called a coward for not "trying harder" or going to marriage counseling. All these people ever saw was two married people living their day-to-day lives—they never knew one of them didn't really want to be there.

People stopped talking to me. My guy friends' wives told them, "Don't talk to him, you'll catch the divorce bug." People I used to have lunch with all the time stopped meeting up with me. People I used to go golfing with stopped making plans with me. People unfriended me on social media. No one wanted to be around me. I even believe part of the reason my law firm partnership dissolved might have been because of my decision to divorce.

I had nobody to talk to. Everybody I knew was gossiping about me behind my back, saying all kinds of crazy things about me and what I was doing. People thought I had gone off the deep end and had turned into some kind of terrible person. They thought I was having a midlife crisis.

It was an incredibly challenging period in my life, and I let it affect me deeply until I realized all the people who chose to abandon me will now miss out on the rest of my life. They listened to what other people said and instead of being true to themselves and being the friends they could have been, they left me behind and now, they will never know me for who I am today.

Though the process was difficult, my divorce taught me that until you are happy first, no one else will be able to make you happy. You have to be whole before anyone else can truly be a part of your life in a meaningful way.

SEEKING HELP

Ending the marriage was not the end of the story. I did not wake up the next day happy and ready for a renewed life. What followed was a grueling three-year period of self-discovery. I had known for years I needed to go to counseling. I knew I was battling some inner demons, but I wasn't doing anything to rid myself of them. I can't tell you how many books I read during the previous decade about professional development and business growth. I can tell you exactly how many I read about battling sadness, mental health, and depression: zero.

But I knew I should not be feeling the way I was feeling. For eight years of my marriage, I would go to bed around 2:30 a.m. and wake up every morning at 6:30 a.m. I couldn't sleep. I had no energy. I was not happy because nothing in my life aligned with what I truly wanted. I thought this unhappiness stemmed from my marriage, but in actuality, it manifested from my practice of internalizing every bad experience in my life to the point of driving myself insane. I needed to regain the power loss I suffered from allowing this to happen over and over in my life. It not only hurt me—now it was hurting everyone else around me.

I found a counselor twenty-five miles away from my house because I didn't want to go to anyone who knew me, and I didn't want anybody to know where I was going. I needed someone I could talk to without any fear of judgment. Because I had no preexisting ties whatsoever to my counselor, I felt at ease to tell him whatever I needed to, and over our sessions, I began to recognize the self-destructive behaviors I was exhibiting that I had never noticed before. For instance, the way I spoke to myself was extremely negative. Oftentimes, when presented with a positive experience or opportunity, the first thing I'd tell myself was, *I'm not worthy of this.* I began to catch myself doing it, and rather than continue down a path of self-destruction, I changed my thought process. When I started feeling unworthy, I would ask myself questions until I landed on an answer I could understand and move past. For example:

Q: Why do you feel this way?

A: Because someone said something racist to me a long time ago.

Q: Have you become successful despite it?

A: Yes, I have.

Q: Why are you letting one comment one person made ages ago control who you are today?

A: Because I haven't let it go.

Q: Can you let it go now?

A: Yes.

As I worked through such issues as needed, the process helped me better understand why I did the things I did. But my real breakthrough came when my counselor asked me the question: who does Luis become when he becomes who God created him to be? That one question took me a month to answer, and when I finally did, it completely changed who I was. Because the answer to the question was simple: when I became who God intended me to be, I became powerful.

I finally understood that to be who I was meant to be, I needed to have power—not power over people, but power over my own thoughts, my own actions, and myself. For too long, I had allowed other people's influence and power to dictate how I was going to feel, how I was going to think, what I was going to believe, and what I was going to do. I no longer wanted the influence of others to dictate my life.

When I told this to my therapist, his next question was: when you become powerful, what life do you live? Again, I took time to consider my answer, visualized a life in which I was totally responsible for my choices, and came to one realization: when I am powerful, I am no longer in my current marriage. In that moment, I knew I had no choice but to live the life I had to live. I wrote my ex a twenty-five-page letter explaining how I came to my decision. It completely devastated her, but it was something I had to do because I could not continue living any other way.

My life has never been the same. I am a totally different human being than I was at that time of my life. I look the same. I sound the same. What's different is the way I feel and the way

I think. My behavior is no longer rooted in fear. I don't behave a certain way because of compulsion or obligation. I truly act the way I act because I want to. I speak the way I speak because I want to. I live the way I live because I want to. It is a very powerful and freeing way to be, and I never take it for granted because I remember being the guy who was scared to make decisions for himself. I remember being terrified of judgment, confrontation, or any negative interaction.

Back then, if I had to fire someone, the stress was unbearable. I'd agonize over everything I planned to say and panic about every possible reaction. I actually started acting hard and tough so others would be afraid to confront me, when really, I was the one who was terrified. Now if I have to fire somebody, I bring them right in and say, "Look. It's not working out. I hate it for you. I hate it for your family. I hate it for us, because I really wanted it to work out, but it's not working out. It's not a reflection of who you are as a person. It's a reflection of our values. We're not aligned in what we want for this company and what you want for the company and for your own self as a professional, so I'm going to give you one week to pack up your things." It's just a matter-of-fact interaction. No, it's not the most pleasant part of my job, but I can do it when necessary and don't doubt my ability to conduct myself in the most professional, respectful manner possible.

It's made me a better, more compassionate leader as well. I once had to discipline an employee who was showing up to work late on a regular basis. Before, I would have just plowed through the conversation, trying to make it end as quickly as possible. In this instance, I took the time to ask what was going on. I found out she was having to drive thirty minutes in the opposite direction of our office to drop her child off at her former mother-in-law's house for childcare. I would never have been able to have that conversation before, because I would have been so scared of what she was going to say. Now, because I was comfortable actually talking to her and getting to the root of the issue, we were able to come to an understanding and resolve it.

Since tapping into my true power, I can walk into any room with no stress or anxiety because I'm not fearful anymore of what anyone else is going to say or do. I know I have the power to be who I need to be, and that's enough.

TURNING THE PAGE

Another way I worked to better myself as I regained my power was by reading. Reading makes you more confident. It gives you new ideas and a fresh perspective. Reading something that resonates with you can change you in ways you can't even imagine. As I mentioned previously, I have no memory for song lyrics, but I can quote some of my favorite book passages by heart. I love pulling quotes from books and using them to encourage or inspire me. I've been an avid reader most of my life, but twice I participated in a reading challenge that I believe helped make me the person I am today.

I did the 52-in-52 Challenge first in 2007 and again after my divorce. I will dive deeper into the specifics of the program and offer my own recommended reading list in Chapter Nine: Next Steps, but for now, I'll tell you the challenge involves reading fifty-two books in fifty-two weeks. I attribute my decision to become a lawyer to the reading I did at that time. The confidence it instilled in me gave me the courage to believe I could attend law school. Law school led me to becoming an attorney, which led me to triple my income.

The second time, I read fifty-five books from May 2017 to

April of 2018. Unlike the first time when I was advancing my career and tripling my income, this time I found myself in a professional rut. My partnership dissolved, my house went into foreclosure, my car was about to get repossessed—and yet I had an incredible attitude. Again, the confidence I gained from reading made me believe everything was going to be okay. By now, you know what happened: I started my own law firm, grew my business, and as of today, have again tripled my income.

READING MAKES YOU MORE CONFIDENT. IT GIVES YOU NEW IDEAS AND A FRESH PERSPECTIVE.

Reading has given me the strength, wisdom, and knowledge to be the best person I can be. My business partner will occasionally say, "I really don't know where you come up with these ideas." I do: I either read about them or was inspired by a book. It might be an amalgamation of ideas from several books. Either way, it's changed how I think, how I act, and how I see the world (again, much more about this to come in Chapter Nine: Next Steps).

CHANGE OF ADDRESS

Finally, my efforts to create the life I wanted led me to the difficult decision to move. I never thought I would leave the west Georgia area. I assumed it was where I would raise my family. But in the wake of all the changes in my life, it was also time for a change of scenery.

Sometimes when you have a fresh mindset and a fresh perspective, the only thing missing is a fresh view. I needed to move to get away from the negativity surrounding me in the area where I lived before I became the person I was meant to be. I needed to put distance between myself and the people who took joy in judging and criticizing me. I didn't want to walk to the store and feel like somebody who couldn't believe what I had done was staring at me anymore. I wanted to live somewhere where I was free, outside of the influence of people who were trying to impact me in a negative way. I knew moving was the best thing for me.

But to do it, I had to sell my house. I had a beautiful 3,000-square-foot home on a one-acre tract of land near a lake. I'd wake up every morning and see the sun rising over the water. It was ideal for holiday decorating, like something out of a Hallmark movie. Basically, it was perfect in every way, and I sold it and moved into a 900-square-foot apartment in Atlanta.

But even though I had to sacrifice the home I loved, I've never been more content. My happiness no longer depends on what I do or what I have. Just the move was refreshing. It helped me feel like I was starting over brand new from the ground up. Plus, living in an apartment being newly married has given both my current wife and me a sense of starting from the beginning. We know we're eventually going to find a house together, maybe get a dog and build a life together. We'll be able to do all those things from the beginning together. Changing my physical perspective completely altered my mental perspective.

SOMETIMES WHEN YOU HAVE A FRESH MINDSET AND A FRESH PERSPECTIVE, THE ONLY THING MISSING IS A FRESH VIEW.

People tend to underestimate the power of finding their own space. The majority of people live within five miles of where their mother lives, the same towns where they were raised and went to high school. It can be nearly impossible to forge your own identity in those places, where everyone expects you to always be the person you were when you were still figuring out what life is all about. I once attended a funeral for a relative of my former business partner where I met many of his friends and family. They all asked me what it was like to work with him. "Is he still that jokester? Man, he's such a prankster," they said. *Prankster?* I thought. He was far from a prankster. I didn't even realize he was funny. He never told a joke. I had never met that version of him, but it was all those people remembered about him. Sometimes, people will continue to project an image of how you were back then onto you, and the only way to escape it is to leave.

COMMITTING TO CHANGE

The only way I was able to come to any of these conclusions or learn any of these lessons was by changing the things in my life that were holding me back from being who I needed to be. As John Maxwell says, "The only way to guarantee that tomorrow's going to be better than today is by growing."

You need to understand that whether you're in a relationship you need to end, in a job you need to move on from, in a business you need to close (or open), if you don't do anything in the meantime, your future is going to be exactly like your past.

If you choose to not do anything differently—whether it's moving, reading, going back to school, or learning a new trade—your life is going to be exactly the same. If you want things to be better, you have to make them better. They're not going to get better on their own. You have to become smarter and make better decisions about the way you think, speak, and act. Change is the only way to gain a new perspective and an inspired mind.

CHAPTER SIX EXERCISES

To start living the life you want, ask yourself:

- What's holding you back from living the life you should be living?
- What are some things you can do to change the reality you're currently experiencing?
- Who are the people you need to consult with to make sure you're making good decisions?

CHAPTER SEVEN

YOU ARE NOT IN CONTROL

FINDING PEACE THROUGH LETTING GO

"The greatest step toward a life of simplicity is to learn to let go."

—STEVE MARABOLI

I have spent a large part of my life being afraid. For a long time, I had a fear of just about anything: flying, roller coasters, being in a car accident, getting mugged. I didn't know it back then, but all these issues could be boiled down to the one thing I feared the most: not being in control.

I went through life constantly trying to control everything around me. Any time I felt out of control, a feeling of desperation would consume me. So, I flew as little as possible. I avoided amusement parks. I always drove myself, even if someone else offered. When I would get home, I would sit in my car until my garage door closed and bolt inside the house to elude the made-up mugger I imagined was lurking nearby. I wanted to control everything about what happened to me in every situation.

When I eventually became a parent, my need to control kicked into overdrive. When my son Ruly entered my life, I decided I had to create an environment for him where I could always know he was safe and secure. I triple-checked every detail of his room, making sure every electrical outlet was covered, every piece of furniture was anchored, no window-blind strings were within reach. I didn't just put a flimsy traditional baby gate at the top of the stairs—I screwed one into the wall, making it a permanent part of the house. As a personal injury lawyer, I know all too well how easily accidents can happen, but I convinced myself all my efforts meant Ruly would always be okay. There was no way he could get hurt—I had made sure of it.

But as any parent will tell you, having kids has a way of shattering your illusion of control and soon enough, life reminded me that hard as I might try, I would never be able to call all the shots. When Ruly was eighteen months old, the family and I were eating dinner at Olive Garden with friends. As usual, Ruly was sitting next to me, and I had cut his food up into practically microscopic pieces. We had all dug into the breadsticks, and suddenly, I looked over at Ruly and saw his face turning bright red. In horror, I realized a piece of bread was lodged in his throat.

As panic coursed through me, I grabbed him, turned him around and started smacking his back. I did not know CPR. I was just trying anything I could think of. People stopped eating and a crowd gathered around us as I continued trying to save him, practically crying from fear, for what felt like an eternity. Frantic as my mind was, I remember one thought pounding through my brain again and again: *I'm going to lose him, and there is nothing I can do about it.*

Someone in the crowd screamed, "Check his throat!" I pried open Ruly's mouth and saw a quarter-sized piece of bread. I jammed my finger as far down his throat as it would go and, unconsciously holding my breath, moved it around until I was able to get the soggy lump out.

Ruly burst into screams, and it was the best sound I'd ever heard in my entire life. I had been convinced I had lost him.

The rest of the evening is a blur. I remember paying and leaving, but all I can remember thinking to myself again and again is, *It doesn't matter how much I try to control my environment, his environment, any environment. There is nothing I can do to prevent something tragic from happening.*

Because the harsh reality is this: we are not in control. No one is—not me, not you, none of us. You can try to avoid it all you want, but you are going to get injured. People you love are going to get hurt. Bad things are going to happen. No life is lived completely devoid of pain. Yet worrying about all those things *will never make your life better.*

While experiencing a moment when I truly thought I might lose my child could have made me even more fearful and desperate for control, I decided instead to view the experience as a reason I should let go and stop letting fear control me. When you live a life aimed entirely at avoiding pain, you're actually living a life of fear. When you live a life of fear, you cannot become who you were created to be, because to do so requires risk, and risk requires you to relinquish control.

I realized my obsession with keeping my son from experiencing harm or negative circumstances was not only bad for me, but it was bad for him. I began to understand if I didn't let Ruly experience falling when he was learning to walk, he'd never know what it's like to get knocked down and get back up again. If he never scrapped his knee when falling off his tricycle, he'd never learn the importance of not letting pain hold you back. My unhealthy obsession with safety had created an environment in which he never learned to fail or, more importantly, to recover.

I also started to see how much damage I was doing to my own emotional state by worrying about things completely out of my control. I needed a different approach. Now, if one of my boys does something I warned them against and gets hurt, I say, "I told you not to do that. That's what happens when you don't listen." The message is not, "That's what you get," but "I hope you learned your lesson because that's what happens when you engage in risky behavior. Those are the consequences. As long as you're okay with those consequences, more power to you, but if you're not okay with those consequences, then you can't behave in that manner." I didn't retreat into being more protective after Ruly's choking incident, because it became so clear to me that pain is required for us to develop into mature and confident people. I knew I needed to provide that opportunity for him, or I was going to end up stifling his growth.

HOW TO GIVE UP CONTROL (AND BECOME MORE SUCCESSFUL IN THE PROCESS)

The first step in giving up control is acknowledging you are not in control. You never have been. You never will be. Yet getting to the point where you realize you're not in control is 90 percent of the battle, because most of us want to feel in control *all the time*. We want to control every situation, every interaction, every detail of our lives. We especially want to micromanage people, and that becomes evident in the way we function in relationships. I have almost 150 employees, all who are upset about another employee at one point or another. When I ask them to explain the problem, it's nearly always rooted in control. Employee 1 did something, Employee 2 reacted a certain way, and now Employee 1 is upset. What they're really saying is, "Their reaction was not in line with what *I* wanted them to do." But really, how often does anyone do exactly what we want them to do?

The truth is no one controls anyone else. If somebody wants to act a certain way, you have no power to change that. You can be an example for others, and you can provide guidance, but you can never control another person's actions. Once you accept that and gain the ability to simply let people be who they are, you'll be far ahead of everyone else in terms of living life to its fullest.

The second way to let go of control is to do the things you find scary. I opted to conquer my fear of heights by riding the Slingshot in Panama City. I voluntarily got into a cage and sat there as two bungees pulled it all the way back to the ground then released and shot me up into the sky. And guess what? I survived. After that, I decided to start flying more often. Doing something that scared me made me realize the things we fear rarely are as bad as we think.

YOU ARE NOT IN CONTROL. YOU NEVER HAVE BEEN. YOU NEVER WILL BE.

By acknowledging I wasn't in control and doing things that scared me, I also was able to reprogram my mind and stop letting fear dictate my choices. Ultimately, the experience taught me that risk and failure—the two main things we assume will come with letting go of control—are not bad things to be feared. By going through such experiences, you are better able to strengthen your character and develop a strong mindset. All the times I failed taught me a valuable life lesson:

- Not making it to the pros taught me there's a life beyond sports.
- Having a partnership that didn't succeed taught me how to find the right partner.
- Having a marriage that didn't succeed taught me the value of being true to myself and speaking up when I know something isn't working.
- Losing a job taught me my entire value isn't in my work.

Each failure and risk taught me a lesson I wouldn't have learned otherwise. I am a firm believer in the saying, "You learn more from doing it wrong and fixing it than you do from doing it right." Failure forces you to figure out how to improve. It's when things don't go right that you can figure out what needs to be done to change it. Without failure, you'd never learn the lessons that are going to help you down the road. In that way, failure and risk actually speed up the process of you becoming successful.

I encourage you to let go of the need to control everything, take more risks, and fail more. Instead of letting fear of risk hold you back, use it to motivate you to become what you were destined to be. Granted, this might seem easier said than done. The fear of failure is so common, there's actually a word for it: atychiphobia. When you have it, the fear is so intense, it restricts you from doing anything at all.

But, in reality, the truly scary thing should not be failure. It should be the certainty that without even trying, you are *guaranteeing you will fail no matter what*. You will go through life never realizing your full potential because you are ensuring your own failure by never taking a single risk.

IT'S TIME TO LET GO OF THE NEED TO CONTROL EVERYTHING, TAKE MORE RISKS, AND FAIL MORE.

DOES IT REALLY MATTER?

Another key to relinquishing control is recognizing the things in your life that actually matter versus the frivolous, unimportant things so many of us spend far too much time worrying about. In the bestselling book *The Subtle Art of Not Giving a F*ck: A Counterintuitive Approach to Living a Good Life*, Mark Manson stresses the importance of only allowing yourself to care about the things that truly matter, primarily the values you hold and the choices you make. Reading his book made me realize how much time and energy I was wasting worrying about what other people thought about me. It mattered what my friends thought about me. It mattered what my family thought about me. It mattered what my coworkers thought about me. It mattered what my partners thought about me. It mattered what people I didn't know thought about me. I even cared about what passing motorists thought about me. I vividly remember driving one day while sipping my coffee drink of choice, a grande caramel latte with an extra shot of espresso from Starbucks, when a car passed me. I actually thought to myself, *I wonder what that person who just saw me drink a Starbucks thinks about me. Do they think I'm cool?* Why was I even *thinking* that? The person probably didn't even see me, and if she did, wouldn't remotely care what I was drinking.

At the time, I did so many things based on how I thought it would make other people see me. I had to have the nicest clothes, the best golf clubs, the coolest car. *The Subtle Art* made me realize I was spending so much time worried about what other people thought about me, when in reality, they probably didn't think about me *at all*. They were just trying to live their own lives. I wasn't so much as a thought in their minds. No one was waking up every morning thinking, *Hey, I wonder what Luis is doing today?* They truly don't care, and I finally understood *I didn't need to either*. The only things I need to care about are my own values, my own choices, and the life I'm living. Once I understood that, I was free.

From that moment on, I didn't have to pretend to be confident—I *was* confident. I didn't have to walk into a room and immediately start stressing about how every other person saw me. I didn't have to be nervous about meeting with an employee. I didn't have to be worked up about meeting with a partner. I didn't have to care because I knew who I was, I knew what my skills were, and I knew what I was worth. I no longer had to worry about what *you* thought about me because I knew what *I* thought about me.

A disclaimer: while *The Subtle Art* did help me greatly in my quest to relinquish control, it was not as easy as reading one book and *boom*, no more issues. The underlying foundation for my ability to change was the preceding ten years when I'd been reading and working toward developing myself, and just like any other behavior change, it took practice. The effortless part was making the decision to no longer allow my need for control to hold me back from becoming the person I wanted to be. I made the decision when I read the book, and I gathered new truth because part of changing your life is replacing the lies you've been telling yourself with what is true. And while that realization was life-changing, it took years for me to reach it. You never know when your breakthrough is going to happen. I had always had a sense I would reach mine; I just didn't know when or how. But I kept reading and kept working through the hardships that came my way, and in the end, everything culminated to mold me into the strong, confident individual I am today.

MORE BLIND SPOTS

The need to control is rooted in fear, and fear is capable of creating blind spots that threaten to derail us as we travel through life. If you don't check your blind spots when driving, you risk running into an approaching vehicle. Sometimes your mirrors aren't enough to see them, because they only reflect whatever is visible from the angle at which they're positioned. If you don't consciously look back and to the side, you're going to miss the semitruck that's coming. Fear acts the same way. If you don't intentionally find the root of your fear, you're going see your life from a limited perspective. You're going to believe nothing is wrong and there's nothing holding you back.

Fear is often the cause of behavior that leads to our suffering, and it can manifest in many different ways. Some people have a fear of never becoming successful. Some people have a fear of becoming too successful. Some people have a fear of losing relationships. Some people have a fear of losing family members. When you find your fear and can identify it, you can recognize when it starts to creep in and impact your thoughts and actions. You're able to look over your shoulder, see fear coming, avoid a catastrophe and keep moving forward.

When I realized my many fears—of dying without making an impact, of not being viewed as successful, of confrontation, of heights, etc.—were keeping me from experiencing life's best, only then could I say, "Fear, you're not going to take ahold of me. I'm not going to let the fear of having this confrontation keep me from having the confrontation. I'm not going to let the fear of heights keep me from flying. I'm not going to let the fear of failing keep me from starting the business." When you find the root of your fear, you can look it in the eye and say, "I'm going to overcome you. I'm not going to allow you to keep me from becoming who I am." Yet many people would rather lie to themselves than confront their fears. They prefer to say, "Oh, I just don't like flying." They use words and phrases to hide the fact that they're actually scared. They'll say things like, "I don't really want to own a business. I just want to make cakes." In reality, they're fearful of what it means to own a business.

For many years, I told myself public speaking was not for me because nobody wanted to hear what I have to say. When I dug deeper, I found an intense fear of rejection. I was terrified people would not like me. I secretly believed I didn't have value to add. But instead of admitting that, I chose to tell myself, "There are already so many speakers out there. I don't need to be another one." Confronting the real fear made me realize there is much to be gained from sharing my life experiences because I can help and inspire people with my words. I no longer let fear stop me from sharing the best of myself with the world.

LOSING CONTROL, FINDING JOY

Knowing who are and owning your identity allows you to relinquish control because you know you can overcome anything. You don't have to control the outcome if you know you can deal with it, no matter what it is. For a long time, I assumed every situation would end in the worst-case scenario, but I know now that's rarely the case. If you have to have a tough conversation with someone, you're not going to die. If someone doesn't like you or see eye to eye with you, it's okay. You are going to find yourself in difficult scenarios and some of them will hurt, but some might turn out better than you ever imagined.

When I realized I had the power to endure anything, there was no reason to be in control of anything. And ultimately, this knowledge led to me becoming a kinder, more loving, happier person. A person who spends his day trying to control everything and perfect his environment lives a life of worry, anxiety, and stress. I can remember staying up until 2:00 a.m. the night before I had to fly worrying about dying. If the earliest flight to any location was 5:00 a.m., I would book it, because I knew I wasn't going to sleep. I always had something to worry about—work, my relationships, how people saw me, anything I could think of. When your mind is consumed completely, it's hard to give anything to anyone else. I was giving so much time and attention to my fear, doubt, anger, anxiety, and depression, I had nothing left to give. It wasn't until I transformed that I could actually pour into other people.

Because you can't love others until you've loved yourself first. You can't be kind to others until you've been kind to yourself first. You can't wish the best for people until you have experienced the best for yourself first. You cannot give what you don't have.

When I tried to give to others without first investing in myself, I was living a double life. On the inside, I felt like I was dying. On the outside, I was playing this role that was never going to be sustainable in the long run. I was completely burned out with people. I wanted to have meaningful relationships, but because I had nothing to give anyone, I was exhausting myself and people were frustrating me. Therefore, I was repelling the thing I wanted. When I finally stopped having—and trying—to control everything and became truly confident in who I was, I began to experience a newness with people. I was able to give and love willingly.

Now, when someone has a great moment or experiences

success, I'm genuinely happy for them. Before, I would think, *I cannot believe that's happening to them. They haven't done anything. I'm over here slaving away and what do I get? Nothing.* I couldn't share in their joy because I didn't have joy in my own heart. Today, because I'm no longer trying to impress anyone, I can be happy with what I have and realize the success of others does not minimize my own. Now I find joy in loving others, wishing the best for them, encouraging them, and helping them access their own power, and it's made me a better friend, husband, father, and leader.

> YOU CAN'T LOVE OTHERS UNTIL YOU'VE LOVED YOURSELF FIRST. YOU CAN'T BE KIND TO OTHERS UNTIL YOU'VE BEEN KIND TO YOURSELF FIRST. YOU CAN'T WISH THE BEST FOR PEOPLE UNTIL YOU HAVE EXPERIENCED THE BEST FOR YOURSELF FIRST. YOU CANNOT GIVE WHAT YOU DON'T HAVE.

WHAT YOU *CAN* CONTROL

While you will never have any power over the vast majority of things in life, there are a few areas where you at least have a say. The first thing you can control is your attitude and the way you choose to act, today and tomorrow. Try as you might, you cannot control anything that has happened in the past. The only thing that can be changed is the future. The most power you have is over the attitude you project into the world as you work each day to be the best version of yourself.

The second thing you can control is what you do with your spare time. I don't mean how you use the hours you devote to your obligations, such as work, kids' activities, or whatever other commitments you have. I mean uncommitted time, no matter how much or how little of it you might have. I believe the bulk of (if not all) of your free time should be dedicated to enhancing your mental state. You should be reading, writing, listening, watching. You should be doing anything that moves you further along to the place where you want to be as a person. Most people don't want to discipline themselves in their spare time. They would rather complain about the things they "can't" achieve in life instead of using those minutes and hours to propel themselves forward. But every human on this planet has the same amount of time in a day. How do you choose to use yours?

Finally, you can control how you treat people. You can control the value systems you follow in your life. You can control your reaction when you feel someone has wronged you. You can control how you respond to the things you can't control. When you control those parts of your life, you end up with a much more fulfilling existence. And when you arrive at this point, your life will become more satisfying.

CHAPTER SEVEN EXERCISES

To make peace with relinquishing control, ask yourself:

- What are the things you are trying to control?
- Can you actually control those things?
- What effect is trying to control those things having on your life?
- What things should you let go of?

CHAPTER EIGHT

NAVIGATING SUCCESS

HOW TO AVOID UNEXPECTED PITFALLS

"Try not to become a man of success but rather a man of value."

—ALBERT EINSTEIN

My first taste of success definitely brought out some of my less attractive qualities. Years later, after I finally became the person I was meant to be, my friends would say, "Man, you used to be so competitive. You would get *so angry* if you didn't win." I don't even remember acting that way—my over-the-top competitiveness was not evident to me at the time because I had not yet discovered who I really was. I just thought I was being a normal person, but really, I was being an annoying jerk.

Now, when I look back at that time of my life, I can't believe I acted that way. My competitiveness manifested even outside the office. I can remember playing a lot of golf at the time, one of the perks of my newfound success. Only I wasn't a great player, and my anger would come out swinging. I'd get mad, bang my club on the ground, take a ball and launch it into the lake. My total lack of self-control was showing itself through immaturity. Success couldn't make me a better golfer. I had more money, better equipment, a better bag, better shoes and clothes—none of it made me more skilled, more patient, or more calm. Instead, it only showed my negative spirit in action.

Once you do become successful—however you define success for you—the great news is that everything else in your life falls magically into place and you never have anything to worry about ever again, right? Wrong! Especially if you haven't yet done the work to figure out who you really are. If you *have* built a foundation rooted in a strong sense of self, you have a much better shot of seeing the pitfalls of success before you're trapped inside them. Either way, challenges are coming, and you'll soon learn success does not make who you are; it only amplifies the qualities you already have.

Professional athletes and entertainers often learn this lesson the hard way. They become successful, then everybody finds out they're not the nicest of people. We've all heard the story of the famous person who spent $10,000 on a dinner and left a $40 tip. That happens because success and wealth doesn't make you generous. It doesn't make you kind. It doesn't make you philanthropic. However, if you already possess all of those desirable qualities, success gives you the opportunity to amplify them. Now, instead of giving $100 to charity, you can give $1 million. Instead of tipping $40, you can tip $1,000.

On the other hand, if you have yet to realize who you truly are at your core, success is going to bring all of the negative things you are to the surface. Lacking a strong sense of self likely will lead you to respond to challenges with sarcasm, anger, pettiness, and passive-aggressiveness. Up until now, some of the more negative qualities you possess might not have been so apparent. But now that you're constantly under scrutiny, a spotlight is shining on them, and you're going to feel like somebody's always criticizing you.

To truly enjoy success, you have to learn to manage it. Think of it this way: If I were to hand you $1 million, I am confident you'd be broke within five years. You'd run through it all because you didn't earn it; it was given to you. You didn't have to go through the grind to get it, and you didn't have to go through the process of figuring out how to become a person who can manage that much money. It's not that you're a terrible person, bad with money, or undeserving. It's simply that until you grow as a person and find out who you truly are, you cannot be responsible for high levels of success. No one can. The performer T-Pain has spoken publicly about how he went from having $40 million in his bank account to $0. He said, "The problem was that I got $40 million before I understood how to manage $1 million." When you have that kind of money, you start thinking, *This amount of money is insane. No one should have this amount of money. And because I don't deserve this amount of money, there's no reason for me not to do whatever I want with it.*

T-Pain bought a $2 million car for himself and houses for his assistant, his mom, and all his cousins, because in his mind, he didn't deserve to have that money anyway. He hadn't gone through the journey of earning it. Having a couple of hits on the radio does not automatically mean you've developed the character you need to maintain and sustain that kind of money. You have to know who you are before you can begin to manage any success that might come your way.

TO TRULY ENJOY SUCCESS, YOU HAVE TO LEARN TO MANAGE IT.

In his book *The Me I Want to Be: Becoming God's Best Version of You*, John Ortberg asserts we can't become the people we want to be because we spend too much time dwelling on the versions of ourselves we *don't* want to be. Instead of activating and self-actualizing, we create inauthentic personas to present to the world because it's safer and easier to be "the me" we think we should be or "the me" other people want us to be. We're afraid to be "the me" God wants us to be, so we go through periods of failure and doubt, worrying more about what other people say and do. Typically, when people say they can't handle the stress of a job, it's because they've never become "the me" they were supposed to be. They can't handle the responsibility that comes with their new life, because regardless of their line of work or where they are in their personal life, more success means more challenges.

And success is not only about the work you do or the money you make. Success is about finding the path that leads to the life you want to live and following it with confidence and conviction day in and day out, day after day after day. You might be perfectly happy in your line of work but want more fulfilling relationships in your personal life. You might be content in your relationships but are always chasing a personal fitness goal you just can't seem to reach. Maybe you want to work on your emotional health, your mental health, your spiritual health. Maybe you already seem to have everything you want on the surface, but inside, you know you are not being true to who you are. Success is about allowing your authenticity to manifest into the life you want to be living. And once you start living that life, certain factors can threaten to derail your focus.

THERE IS NO FINISH LINE

Many people tend to see reaching a certain level of success as the end of their struggle. They think, "I did all the work. Now I'm here and I can just sit back and enjoy it." But in truth, when you reach the level of success you were striving to achieve—again, no matter what that "success" looks like for you—that's when the real journey really begins. You need to be who you are meant to be so the responsibility and pressure that comes with success doesn't overtake you.

There's a saying about "being on the other side of the promise," which refers to when Moses led Israel to the Promised Land. It means you've arrived, but the truth is, once you're on the other side of the promise, your work is just getting started. When the Israelites got to the Promised Land, they had to fight. The rest of the Old Testament is about them fighting war after war with other tribes and cultures. Your Promised Land might be becoming a successful business owner, artist, entertainer, or athlete. It might be becoming a better parent, sibling, friend, or spouse. No matter what it is, once you get there, you will have to fight to keep it. For example, getting someone to enter into a relationship is not the hard work—maintaining a healthy relationship is what matters. You can't just focus on the big, exciting moments or milestones. You have to pay attention to the little details, the things that add up at the end of each day to create the life you are living together. I once heard someone say that while the flashy new attraction is always what draws people to Disney World, the trash cans keep them there. Disney is so focused on attention to detail, even the trash cans are unique in different parts of each park. In Tomorrowland, they're shaped like spaceships. In Animal Kingdom, they're little huts. In Toy Story Land, they're (you guessed it) toys. Those little touches make those parks what they are: widely appealing, painstakingly consistent, and extremely successful.

Your fight to maintain success will require you to continuously grow and learn. One of the things I love about my business partner is, regardless of what level of success we achieve, he never stops working toward a new goal. When I first started working with him, he told me his aim was to sign twenty new clients a day. If we hit that mark, he said, he would finally relax. Eighteen months later, twenty new clients a day is standard, and revenues have increased tenfold. I asked him, "Are you going to relax now?" He said, "And risk going backward? No way!" He understands the work in maintaining success is not about reaching the pinnacle; it's about staying there. If you tell yourself success is a destination, you're going to be crushed when you get there and realize it's nowhere near as freeing as you anticipated.

SOCIAL MEDIA MYTHS

Social media has done nothing to convince anyone that success requires a great deal of work to maintain. We see someone like Grant Cardone, who owns four thousand rental properties and runs a consulting business that makes $100 million a year, flying around the country on his private jet, and it seems like he's always vacationing. We see someone like Kim Kardashian and think she doesn't have to "work" a day in her life. We read about Tom Brady having multiple personal chefs and personal trainers. But what we don't realize is those people probably work harder than any of us do.

After twenty years in the NFL, Brady is still working his butt off every day, because he knows there's another twenty-two-year-old kid coming out of college who wants to take his position. He knows success is not about arriving in the NFL or signing that first contract—he knows it's about continuing to work as hard as you did before you had it because every success you achieve is just a stepping stone to the next level.

Furthermore, when we see the flashy lifestyles celebrities present, we automatically assume that means they are happy. We assume all their relationships are healthy, all their problems magically solve themselves, and all their fears and anxieties are nonexistent. But they are people just like the rest of us, and simply being well-known because of what they do for a living does not guarantee success in every area of their lives.

THE PITFALLS

No matter how you define success, there are a few common traps you will be tempted to fall into once you've reached a certain level. I have experienced each of these firsthand and hope in detailing them here, I can help you avoid making similar mistakes. A disclaimer: most of these do pertain to my professional experiences but I believe the lessons learned are applicable to many areas of life.

RELYING ON CHARISMA OVER CHARACTER

Many outgoing people fall victim to this. These are the people who light up the room. They're bubbly; they smile a lot. Entertainers are often in this camp. The danger comes, however, when these people start relying on those qualities as a means of maintaining success. Charisma is capable of taking you places your character cannot sustain.

If you are naturally charismatic, it's likely you were the most popular kid in school. You were probably active in student government, theater, and/or athletics. Maybe you were on the homecoming court. When fitting in and getting the things you want comes naturally to you, it's easy to not become a better person. Everybody already thinks you're great, so why change? Now you're relying on something you didn't earn.

Think of people who lose weight through very quick means: liposuction, a thirty-day cleanse, some fad diet. The next thing you know, they're gaining it all back, because they didn't earn it. They have no reason to maintain healthy habits because they didn't go through the long journey and the grind to achieve the weight they wanted (I understand this is not always the case, but for a majority of people, it is). Charisma works the same way. If you don't work to develop your character, you're going to become selfish because everything will always be all about you. Yes, you might be able to sell anything or attract thousands of social media followers, but you are not becoming the person you are meant to be. You are not becoming more kind, generous or loving, and your charisma will become your downfall.

You have to work harder at developing your character so you can maintain the aspects of your personality that attract people to you in the first place. Long-lasting qualities such as integrity, respect, and authenticity will take you farther than charm ever will.

BECOMING COMPLACENT

The most common cause of complacency is lost passion. Lost passion is the killer of careers and the destroyer of relationships. The second someone feels they no longer have to work at a relationship, they are in danger of losing it. Any time I hear someone say, "So-and-so and I are such good friends, we could be apart for a year and pick right back up like no time has passed at all," I always think, *Wow, you really must not care about so-and-so.* The question is why did you allow a whole year to pass without seeing them? What caused you to become so complacent in that relationship that you became fine basically never seeing them? People in successful relationships are not complacent—they seek each other out and make sure they are giving that relationship its best chance at success.

Unfortunately, complacency is widespread in the workforce. According to our firm's client advocate, who works to develop our workplace culture, people tend to lose interest in any job within 120 days of being there. They start off excited to learn and grow, but 120 days in, they're just working. The problem is we have become creatures of entertainment. We constantly need to be entertained, inspired, motivated, recharged.

It's the reason people no longer stay in jobs for their entire careers. They're not passionate about anything, so they're working jobs simply to cover their needs in the short-term. One of my employees who studied millennial psychology said most young people today don't even think about retirement and won't until they near retirement age. All they're thinking about is how they can accomplish their immediate personal goals today. If they want to travel the world, for instance, they don't want to wait until they are older to do it. Rather than getting a job, climbing the ladder, saving money, and accruing vacation time, they determine how many months they have to work the job they currently have so they can make enough money to travel right now. Those two weeks in Italy makes working a job they don't love worth it to them.

When you are passionate about what you do, the idea of doing anything else seems absurd. But you risk losing that passion if, once you reach a certain level of success, you decide you can rest on your laurels and stop seeking inspiration or setting new goals. You should always be aiming to reach the next level, whatever that may be.

I'm not saying success requires being trapped in a never-ending cycle of chasing the next thing. You absolutely can enjoy the rewards of all the hard work you've done. But if you become complacent and lose passion, you risk losing your true identity because now you're no longer continuing to self-actualize.

You have to do things to reactivate your passion and reenergize yourself, which can be challenging, especially when no one else is cheering you on. I have found that when you start a business or embark on a new endeavor, everyone's really happy for you. But once you've been at it for a long time and become successful, people aren't as encouraging. When I started my own law firm, people were coming out of nowhere to give me cases. Fast-forward to current day, when a friend of mine told me he doesn't send me any cases because I "have enough." People are not as supportive as you get more successful, and you'll find you have to encourage yourself. But that's okay, because no one is going to be a bigger cheerleader for you than you.

> **WHEN YOU ARE PASSIONATE ABOUT WHAT YOU DO, THE IDEA OF DOING ANYTHING ELSE SEEMS ABSURD.**

RIDICULE AND PERSONAL ATTACKS

In a world full of anonymous quotes and comments, it is so easy for someone to say something negative and not be held accountable for it. When you are becoming successful, everyone—even friends and family—are going to criticize, ridicule, or attack you in one form or another, and there's no way to avoid it. Some people are going to do it simply because they just don't like you regardless of whether they actually know you or not.

When I first came onto the firm, there was an employee (who shall remain nameless) who didn't know me. I had only been at the job a week or two, and we had never spoken or spent any time together. I was just trying to learn and figure out what my role was. Out of nowhere, this employee resigned. No two-week notice, no heads-up; he just quit. My business partner asked him for an explanation, and the now–ex employee requested I be present when he made his statement.

In the meeting, he pointed right at me and said, "I'm resigning because of you."

"I've seen you here," he said to me. "You've been here two weeks, and not one time have you offered to take me to lunch. Not one time have you even said anything but hello to me. Not one time have you asked me about my family. Not one time have you asked me about my kids. You don't care about anybody here."

I was shocked. I was being personally attacked because of an expectation he had of me that I didn't fulfill, one he never even communicated to me. It made no sense to me whatsoever, but I could tell there was no reasoning with him, so he left.

I later found out he had assumed he was going to run the firm one day and saw me as the guy preventing him from becoming the future manager. My partner had never given him reason to believe such a plan was in place, but he had convinced himself it was true and was therefore operating from a place of misinformation and delusions of grandeur. It didn't matter who had my role—he was going to quit no matter what. The fact that he didn't even know me didn't matter.

It's worse, perhaps, when the attack comes from someone who does know you, albeit the old you, not the new you. As you go through your period of self-discovery, you're going to find that people always latch on to the last you they knew. People who only knew me when I was chasing success still call me competitive, argumentative even. It's true I used to argue a lot, but I don't anymore. That version of me doesn't exist anymore, but people still use that time of my life to try to box me in.

Anyone who is jealous of you is going to attack you for anything and everything possible. People have ridiculed my firm's billboards, our social media presence, our TV commercials, our radio ads. These are people who know of us, and they think that means they can say whatever they want about what we do.

Finally, there will be people who know you who just don't want you to be successful. These can be hard to spot. They're the "friends" who are kind to your face, but behind your back, they're gossiping about you, spreading rumors and negativity. You have to be careful around these people, because more often than not, they act like they genuinely care about you, but they actually only want to bring you down because of what you represent. Your success only shows them what they haven't been able to achieve in their own lives. People tend to compare themselves to the most successful person in their circle, and if that's you, watch out. I remember when I was in law school, I had a lot of friends who would discourage me from studying. "You can do that later," they'd say. "You don't have to be disciplined. Come out with us tonight. Let's go to the game. Let's go to a party." That's not a supportive thing to say to a person who's in law school. But studying represented the discipline they lacked in their own lives. They weren't working toward becoming great, and they didn't want me to either. Years later, I've learned that eventually, your haters always end up talking about how they knew you and when. Now that they can see me on billboards and in TV commercials, all those people who didn't like the fact that I was so disciplined then love to talk about how they know me now.

I found the best way to combat all this negativity was to identify the friends who were genuinely supportive of me and who wanted the best for me. It wasn't a lot of people—just a handful of those who always checked on me, who encouraged me to get to the next level, who prayed for me, who shared in my joy when my dreams became a reality. If such people aren't emerging organically in your life, I suggest you go looking for them. Find an entrepreneur support group. Join a networking organization. Enroll in a mentoring program. Creating a team of people who will support you in a variety of ways will shield you from those who try to personally attack you.

LETTING RESPONSIBILITY OVERWHELM YOU

Again, many people underestimate the amount of responsibility success really entails. And because they underestimate it, they're not prepared for it, and the shock can undo all the great work they've done to that point.

When you become a person of great influence, you take on more responsibility in every aspect of your life. As a business owner, I have to be careful what I post on social media. Political rants or opinionated comments have no place in my posts. I have to be careful how I present myself in any situation. Even a minor display of road rage could ruin my reputation. I have to be careful about how I dress. In the city of Atlanta with its seven million people, I routinely see people I know, so bumming around in sweats is not an option.

That level of responsibility can be overwhelming, because there is no escaping it. And if your character does not strengthen as your success grows, you're going to find yourself acting out of desperation, which eventually can lead to your demise as a professional. Just look at Antonio Brown, the NFL player who lost $30 million because he didn't want to wear a certain helmet. He alleged the helmet would limit his vision and interfere with his performance, but instead of approaching the situation logically and reasonably, he started acting out. He didn't show up to training camp. He was rude to his coaching staff and teammates. He was eventually traded then let go when allegations started to surface about sexual misconduct in his past. He lost millions because he couldn't live up to the responsibility of being an NFL football player. When you become successful, the responsibility is greater because the potential loss is greater.

One key to avoid feeling overwhelmed is to develop a keen ability to prioritize. When I first became the managing attorney of the firm, I found the position daunting. I didn't really know what I needed to do. Do I cash checks, sign checks, write policies and procedures, organize meetings? I had no idea, but rather than start making rash and potentially unwise decisions, I made myself think rationally. I asked myself, *What are the things I can do that no one else can? What tasks can be delegated?* Answering those simple questions helped me understand what I was supposed to do, and I was able to start giving commands.

Delegation is easier for some than others, but it's important to be able to recognize there are some things you simply don't need to do. One attorney I knew (who earns $300,000 a year, by the way) just moved into a new house and did not hire a moving crew. He wanted to save the $1,200 cost and opted to spend an entire three days moving himself. During those three days, he was completely overwhelmed trying to juggle work and the move, when he could have just signed a check and moved on with his life. Gaining the ability to determine which responsibilities are better assumed by someone else can be life changing.

On your journey to becoming the person you are meant to be, you are going to see other people who have not worked as hard as you reach their goals faster. I experienced this on a personal level. When I was working for the old firm and simultaneously going to law school in my twenties, I was hustling round the clock. I would start my workday at 5:00 a.m., sometimes even earlier if I was meeting with an injured client who worked the night shift. I poured my blood, sweat, and tears into chasing my dream of becoming an attorney.

In his twenties, my brother was basically goofing off, earning a 2.3 GPA while he got his chemistry degree, spending much of his time partying, hanging out with friends, or traveling. But I always tried to encourage him to do more with his life, and eventually, I hired him to be a legal assistant at my firm. He worked for me for five years, during which he kept partying, going to clubs, and basically focusing on fun. But I kept pushing him to do more, and at the age of thirty, he decided to become a real estate agent. In a matter of four years, he developed his real estate business to the point he is earning over $500,000 a year. He bought a $1 million dollar home. He and his wife have been able to pay off all of their debt. They're saving and investing. He's banked millions.

I admit I had to take a moment to come to terms with that. I spent all of my twenties grinding and granted, I'm successful, but he became *really* successful without the sacrifice. He had outgrown me in the sense that he didn't need me pushing him to be more—he *was* more, and he had surpassed me, at least monetarily (though to be clear, I caught up. LOL.).

Of course, I'm very excited for him and his family but I can acknowledge there was something inside of me that resented the fact that I suffered while he seemed to not care about his own future. Seeing his success made me question some of the decisions I'd made in my own life. I started falling into the pit of comparison, and it took me some time to realize his success had nothing to do with me or my own life. When someone outgrows you, it's natural to analyze the similarities and differences in the paths you've both taken. But it's critical to remember that the success of someone else does not take away from your own.

My musician brother-in-law is the perfect example of this. A few years ago, he decided to try to make it in Nashville. Despite the people who laughed at him or predicted his failure, he did what he felt he needed to do. He moved, started booking gigs in bars, met some people, and today, he's writing with performers whose songs have millions of streams online. Too many people, when they see others enjoying success, start to believe their own efforts aren't worth it. But if you stay committed, you learn that the work itself is worth it, as long as it's something you feel passionate about, and it allows you to continue to grow as a person. The reason many people who appear on shows like *American Idol* or *The Voice* go on to do exactly nothing is because they don't work to develop themselves into someone who can add value to the music industry. They can sing, sure, but that's a talent they were born with. It's like charisma—if that's all you have, you're a goner. But if you develop yourself into an entertainment professional—learn how to write music, play an instrument, produce—you become valuable. As long as you're bettering yourself, you never have to worry about other people outgrowing you because you are still growing yourself.

Success does not boil down to a mathematical equation. It's not as if every time someone takes a piece of the pie, there's one less piece left for you. The truth is we all have our own pie, and there is no limit to how much pie can exist in the world. You can even bake new pies. If that wasn't true, companies such as

Apple or Facebook never would have succeeded. But instead of focusing on our own pie, we spend time worrying about how much other people have. We say, "If that person is becoming successful in my job, that means there's no other place for me to go." I once had an employee who wanted to become management complain to me that no positions were available. I pointed out to her that our firm was growing every day. That growth meant more employees. More employees meant the need for more managers. She was dumbfounded. I encouraged her to keep working hard and developing herself into a person who can be a manager. The opportunity will be there—she just needs to be ready for it.

SUSTAINING SUCCESS BY KNOWING YOURSELF

When you truly know who you are, charisma won't be your guide. Your character, integrity, and authenticity will shepherd you through any situation. When you know who you are, you can't become complacent, because operating outside of anything other than your passion simply doesn't make sense. When you know who you are, ridicule and personal attacks have no impact on you because you know who you are, and when someone questions that, it's merely a reflection of their own insecurities.

When you know who you are, you won't feel overwhelmed by responsibility. You know how to prioritize and delegate. When you know who you are, you won't worry about the growth of other people, because you know there is a plan for you. You know who you were created to be and that there is a pathway for your success.

No matter what goal you have for yourself, you never have to worry about how other people live. You only have to be worried about the person you were created to be and how you can continue to work to become the best version of that person possible. When you do that, you maximize your capacity for joy because not only are you finding happiness in your own success, but you also can genuinely share in the elation of those around you who are following their own paths to prosperity.

CHAPTER EIGHT EXERCISES

To make sure you are prepared to navigate success:

- Identify the areas in your life where you feel yourself becoming complacent.
- Identify the triggers that are stopping you from moving forward in life.
- Identify the responsibilities that are capable of making you feel overwhelmed, and think about how you can reprioritize them.
- Identify what makes you sit back and relax on your success.
- Finally, take steps to create the discipline in your life so that you do not take your success for granted.

CHAPTER NINE

NEXT STEPS

BEGINNING YOUR JOURNEY TO SUCCESS

"Faith is taking the first step even when you can't see the whole staircase."

—MARTIN LUTHER KING JR.

As you embark on the path of self-discovery that will lead you to becoming the person you are meant to be, you will soon learn there are no shortcuts. There is no easy fix for overcoming the obstacles in your path. There is no get-rich-quick scheme that will propel you to success. It takes a great deal of work, time and effort. I once heard someone say it took them ten years to become an overnight success, because while everyone sees the fruits of your labor, few know what it truly took for you to get there. My own journey took fifteen years. I started in the legal industry in 2004, didn't realize what I was truly good at until 2016, and began managing my own firm in 2019.

While I know what activities and tactics were helpful for me along the way, there is no one formula of success that will work for every person. But as you start your journey, I encourage you to at least try all of the recommendations suggested in this chapter, even if it's outside of your comfort zone or something that simply doesn't appeal to you, as you never know where it might lead you. I have found if you do these things, you are much more likely to find the passion inside of you that will lead you to the life you are meant to live. There also is no wrong way to go about it—whatever works for you is the right thing to do. The most important thing you can do is get started.

READING

Reading has the power to reshape the way you think. One of my dad's favorite biblical phrases is Romans 12:2: "Do not conform to the pattern of this world, but be transformed by the renewing of your mind." Many of us live lives of conformity. We just accept our circumstances—where we live, where we went to school, where we work, who we associate with—and never do anything with intention. We don't *choose* anything. You likely didn't choose what high school you went to; you didn't choose what friends were available to you. You may have chosen your college, but it might have been a choice of convenience because of location or cost. You likely didn't choose your first job as it was probably the first one offered to you. You didn't even choose your own name—your parents gave it to you.

Reading renews the mind and helps you learn to act intentionally. You have to make the conscious decision to be transformed so you can change your circumstances, and one of the best ways to transform is to read. Reading gives you words that can change your mindset and alter your attitude.

It's easy to come up with reasons not to read. Some avoid it because of the commitment it requires. You have to dedicate time to reading—you can't be doing anything else while you're engaged with a book. You need an environment free of distractions. Some people don't want to spend money on books (though allow me to remind you the library is free). They'll buy a drink that costs $16, whereas if they'd spent that money on a book, it might have taught them how to increase their income by $16,000. We invest money in things that don't give us any return—clothes, shoes, fancy dinners—instead of investing in ourselves.

People also tend to underestimate the power of reading. In all societies where people are oppressed, books are outlawed. In North Korea, they outlaw the Bible. In Cuba, they outlaw books about capitalism. Slaves were denied access to books. Yet today, we have thousands of books available to us, and people willfully choose not to read. And worse yet, we have "gurus" out there professing that reading is meaningless. That all you have to do is take action. But tell that to the kid who has suffered emotional insecurity for twenty years and see how easy it is for him to "just take action." Reading can show that same kid how the entire world is open to him. Reading is a portal to finding the life you want for yourself. It unlocks the secrets of life. Reading helps you alter your negative programming so that you can actually take action. For some, that reprogramming might take a couple of books; for others, it might take hundreds. But mark my words, those who read will find success.

If you find reading intimidating, think of it like going to the supermarket: you're not going to buy every single item, only the things you want. You're not going to take every single lesson from every single book. You're just going to take what you need. But you don't really know what you need until you start reading. Whenever I pick up a book, I'm never sure what I'll take away from it. But I do know if I never pick it up, I'll never find out. Remember, there's no wrong way to do it.

Twice in my life, I participated in a personal challenge to read fifty-two books in fifty-two weeks. Both times, I experienced personal, professional, and financial growth beyond what I could ever have imagined. During the course of both challenges, within twenty-four to thirty-six months, I more than doubled my income because reading gave me the knowledge and confidence to become the person I needed to be. I believe any person who takes the time to read fifty-two books in fifty-two weeks will develop such intense discipline, receive such significant takeaways, and transform their thinking in such massive ways that within twenty-four to thirty-six months of finishing, if they implement what they took away, they will grow their income by double or maybe even much more.

I know there is someone out there thinking this is not necessary. There is someone out there who can point to dozens of people who have not read anything and became successful. It's true this approach is not right for everyone. If you are already living in your purpose and are as successful as you want to be and have everything you want to have, you may not need to do this. That doesn't negate the fact that this process will work, and I have seen it work many times in my own life and in the lives of other people I coach and mentor.

PEOPLE TEND TO UNDERESTIMATE THE POWER OF READING.

If you're not already a reader, don't stress about plowing through a book a week. Just start with ten minutes a day. I suggest doing it early in the morning so your mind is fresh and you can check it off your to-do list before even starting your day. Don't get frustrated if you go slowly. Just start reading and your stamina will grow.

I believe everyone should read three different types of books:

1. Self-help. These books are going to give you practical knowledge, tips on how to overcome the things you're dealing with, ways to help you understand yourself better, and tools you can use to become a better person. They will make you a more strategic thinker and a better leader and coworker.

2. Anything related to emotional intelligence. Books related to spirituality, religion, or the human condition can help you better understand yourself and the world around you. These books will help you read the room and become a better networker and relationship builder. Relationships are key to becoming ultra-successful.

3. Autobiographies or biographies of successful people. These books help you understand other people's journeys and show you how though we're all struggling to find our own way, and everyone has a different path, everyone can get there. They will show you the pitfalls these people faced so you can avoid them but also show you where they were able to shrink time in their journey, so you can too.

For specific titles, check out my recommended reading list in the appendix.

FINDING A COACH

As you grow into the person you are meant to be, you need someone who can guide and encourage you. It helps if it's someone who has more life experience than you, someone older who has been there and can help you along the way. Coaches are mentors who make you see the things you're doing wrong, help you avoid future mistakes, and elevate you to heights you could never reach alone.

I've had three coaches in my life to whom I attribute much of my success. The first one is a judge I met when I was nineteen years old. He taught a class I took as an undergrad and when he found out I aspired to become an attorney, he offered me an internship opportunity. I worked in the magistrate court, state court, superior court, and traffic court, and with the solicitor and district attorney. I went on a ride along with the police department. I delivered warrants with the sheriff's department. I worked in the jail, with the probation officers, and with a criminal defense attorney. The experience completely changed the trajectory of my life as it gave me the confidence I needed to go to law school. Twenty years later, we're still friends and he remains an amazing mentor of mine.

My second coach was a family friend and business owner who I met in my early twenties. He took me under his wing and would bring me along to meetings and business dinners and generally show me the ropes of running a successful business. The tips and tricks I learned from him are still things I do today. For instance, he taught me you should never wear your jacket while you're riding in the car because it gets wrinkled. You should hang it up in the back seat. Then, when you arrive, retrieving it gives you time to take a breath before the meeting. Plus, you never know if somebody's going to come out to meet you or watching you from the window, and nothing makes you appear more calm and collected than taking the time to put on your jacket after getting out of your car. You look confident and ready for anything. He also taught me to never sit with my back to the door in a conference room because you want to be able to see the person you're meeting with as they arrive. You should look them in the eye and welcome them into your space. These little lessons and many more like them have stuck with me throughout my career and made a difference in how I handle myself in any professional setting.

My third coach, my dad, has been by my side, cheering me on my entire life. Having read this far, you know by now the impact he's had on nearly every aspect of my life. He has given me the foundation and guidance I needed to become the person I was meant to be.

There is no wrong way to find a mentor. I encourage you to seek out people in your own life who can help you in similar ways. Who are the people who bring out the best in you? Who can help you as you navigate the path to success? Maybe it's a friend, neighbor, pastor, or teacher you already know. Maybe it's someone you've yet to meet at a conference or networking event. Once you find that person, rely on their guidance, wisdom, and support as you continue your mission of growth. If no one comes to mind, remember that paying for a coach or mentor is an option. I currently pay three different professional business coaches who are tasked with helping me maintain a healthy, positive mindset as I navigate the ups and downs of business ownership. They offer me unique insight and perspective, and the guidance and support they provide is invaluable. If you are in a position to pay someone to help you in this area, there truly is no excuse for not having a mentor.

If the help you need is more serious, I also encourage you to seek out a professional counselor. When I was experiencing bouts of depression and lacking the confidence I needed to become the person I wanted to be, the decision to find a counselor changed my life for the better in ways I never could have anticipated. Working with someone who was able to pinpoint my blind spots and help me overcome them allowed me to free myself. My counselor gave me the tools I needed to self-actualize and become my true, authentic self.

SEEKING INSPIRATION

We all know what it feels like to be hungry; we all know what it feels like to be satisfied. Our minds work the same way. There are times when our minds crave to be filled with something new. Engaging with something motivational on a consistent basis helps satiate your mind while giving you the confidence to know you can bring value to any situation. Since beginning my habit of reading, listening to, or watching something motivational every day, I've become more balanced, stable, and even-keeled.

If you don't know where to start, simply go to YouTube and type in the word "motivation" or "inspiration." Click through the videos until you find one that resonates with you. I gravitate to any video featuring one of my favorite speakers, Les Brown, who tends to focus on our ability to contribute to the world and how to be intentional about being meaningful. If that appeals to you, there are no shortage of his videos available.

Podcasts are another great source for finding inspiration. As you begin reading, find out if any of your favorite authors have one. Listen to how they speak and determine if becoming a regular listener could add value to your life.

Conferences can be powerful motivators. I'm an avid conference goer, and there have been several when I've left feeling like I could walk through a wall. When you go to a conference and hear perspectives of other people, it changes the way you see the world. A change in perspective can be more important than an increase in knowledge. When you change the way you look at things, everything you look at begins to change.

When it comes to finding inspiration on a regular daily basis, there is no wrong way to explore a new source or wrong time to do it. The right source is the one you find most engaging. The right time is whenever you can commit to doing it. If you're a morning person, do it as soon as you wake up. If you're a night owl, do it right before going to sleep. There's no one-size-fits-all way for you to grow and for you to change your life. Furthermore, if you try something and it doesn't work for you, it's okay to move on. There is no reason to waste time engaging with something that isn't advancing you on your journey.

If the idea of introducing one more thing to your daily routine seems daunting, start small. Read one page. Watch a video for one minute. The goal is not to read for some arbitrary period of time—the goal is to consume words that can change your perspective, and that can happen in an instant. You could read one page that completely changes how you think. If you read consistently, you'll be more likely to find the thing that will have a profound impact on you, so if you can do one minute a day, try to graduate to two, then five, then ten until you are doing it for genuine pleasure.

THERE ARE TIMES WHEN OUR MINDS CRAVE TO BE FILLED WITH SOMETHING NEW.

If you're listening to something, such as a podcast or TED Talk, there's nothing to stop you from incorporating it into your daily life. Put it on while you're brushing your teeth and making breakfast. Listen to it on your drive to work, during lunch, at the gym, anywhere. The more you incorporate it into your daily life, the more value you'll find in it.

In addition to Les Brown, some of my favorite speakers include:

- Gary Vee
- Eric Thomas
- Hal Elrod
- Rachel Hollis
- Jen Sincero
- Tony Robbins
- Priscilla Shirer
- Myles Munroe
- Jim Rohn
- Suze Orman
- Jennie Allen
- Jen Hatmaker
- Dave Ramsey
- Jon Acuff
- Jack Canfield
- Zig Ziglar
- Wayne Dyer
- Simon Sinek
- Grant Cardone

ASSOCIATING WITH THE RIGHT PEOPLE

A business mentor of mine once said, "Where you are in five years is going to be based on the books you read, the people you listen to, and the people you hang around with." A key part of leveling up in life is surrounding yourself with people who have the same vision and are on the same path as you.

Many of us spend time with people who bring us down and who don't add value, not realizing the emotional toll it takes on us. All of us have that one friend who is overly negative or that one family member whose world is always crashing down. The more we interact with such people, the more they are able to affect us. I never want to hang out with a Debbie Downer. If someone is always talking about how their life sucks, how they can never make any money, how terrible their job is, I do not want to be anywhere near them. Negative self-talk keeps people operating at low levels, and I'm not interested in participating in that in any way. Some people are just nasty. If I meet somebody who is constantly criticizing others and never has a nice thing to say, I know it's very likely they're saying the same things about me when I leave the room. I don't want anything to do with that person.

As mentioned before, it can be particularly difficult if the most negative people in your life are also members of your family. You obviously can't totally weed them out, but you also can't continue to allow them to bring you down. Remember that not everybody is entitled to the best of you, especially if they don't give you the best of them. I suggest you stop sharing your big ideas with those people. You can still love them and spend time with them, but if you're also sharing your innermost dreams and goals with them, all you're doing is hurting yourself.

There is power in associating with people who can uplift you and add value to your life, and doing so may require you to change your social circles. Reach out to people who are on the same trajectory as you. If you want to be successful in a particular field, associating with people who already are established and thriving can help you get the knowledge and connections you need. View every step you take as an opportunity to meet those people. You'd be surprised how it can happen just by living your ordinary life in a way that attracts like-minded people. An easy way to start is by exuding as much positive energy as you can in any situation. Be kind to everyone you meet. Be generous with your time, your money, your mind, and your resources. If you want to surround yourself with people who are like you,

you have to become the type of person other people want to be around, and when you begin to add value to other people, they naturally want to engage with you.

I do this by sharing my ideas with others. Spreading knowledge and helping others learn from my own experiences is how I chose to contribute. As a result, I've been asked to consult with people about their businesses. I've booked speaking engagements. I've met many well-connected people simply because I have been willing to give of myself. You too can begin to attract the people you want in your life by being generous with your own time and knowledge.

Another way to attract like-minded people is to simply lead an active life and engage in as many activities as possible. In other words, turn off the TV and get out into the world. Join a group aimed at a hobby or activity you love (I'm on a kickball team). Go to every networking event you can find. Accept dinner party invitations. Attend local sporting events. There is no wrong way to meet someone—simply view each event as an opportunity.

WRITING DOWN YOUR GOALS

Every day, several times a day, I take the time to write down the things I want most in life. It helps me stay on track and align my mind with how I plan to achieve my goals. Writing down your dreams helps affirm the steps you're taking to reach them.

It's key to make sure your goals have action attached to them. If I say I want washboard abs, but I don't actually go to the gym or eat healthy, then it's just a fantasy. I'm never going to achieve it. So, rather than writing down the end goal, it helps to write down the steps you need to take to get there. In this example, my goal is not to get washboard abs; the result is washboard abs. My goal is to go to the gym every single day. Instead of saying, "My goal is to make $10,000," you should write down, "My goal is to show up to work and be the best employee I can possibly be." When you do that, you position your mind to achieve something you've never achieved before.

Don't expect this exercise to make your goals manifest instantaneously. When I was twenty-six, I filled fifty pages of a journal writing the same goal again and again: "I earn $1 million per year." I did not achieve that goal until ten years later. But the dedication to the goal I had back then is what led me to the place I am in today.

I write down all of my financial goals, all of my relationship goals, all of my business-related goals. And because there's no wrong way to do it, sometimes what I write down are not goals I strive to achieve but aspects of my life I want to maintain. For example, I might write, "I have a thriving business," "I have a great relationship with my business partner," "I am happily married," or "I have great kids." Those are all true, but when I write them down, it repositions my mind so I continue to reaffirm my understanding of such things. Then when my kids act up, I remind myself through my subconscious that I really do have great kids. If I'm presented with a business challenge, I know my firm is successful. I never question the things I know to be true because I remind myself of them every day.

I usually write down ten to fifteen goals every day, three times a day: morning, afternoon, and evening. In the morning, it helps me get my mind right. Midday, it helps me keep my mind right. At night, it helps me go to bed with a positive mindset.

The best thing about all of these next steps is you can start them right now. They don't require anyone else's help. All it takes is for you to make the decision that today is the last day you're going to stop yourself from getting the things you want. Today is the day you're going to change your perspective through reading. Today is the day you're going to associate with better people. Today is the day you're going to listen to something that's motivational. Today is the day you're going to find a coach. Today is the day you're going to write down your goals.

As soon as you start making these changes, you will see true change in your life, and you'll become more confident and motivated as you move closer to becoming the person you were meant to be. There is no reason to put the journey off until tomorrow. Start today.

CHAPTER NINE EXERCISES

To get started on your next steps:

- Write down the first book you're going to read.
- Compile a list of three people you consider a possible coach or mentor and reach out to them.
- Make a list of the authors, speakers, or podcasters you want to look into as possible sources of inspiration.
- Ask yourself, who are the "right" people you should be associating with? Who are the "wrong" people you should no longer associate with?
- Write three specific goals you want to achieve in the next twelve months.

CONCLUSION

Through the course of reading this book, you've probably questioned why you've had to endure all of the challenges and hardships in your life. You might have experienced relationship challenges, job challenges, or financial challenges and feel as if life has been one difficulty after another, all seemingly keeping you from doing the things you want to do and becoming the person you want to become. But I want you to know no matter what you've been through, it's all been for a reason. Because *life has to hurt.*

For in those moments of true pain, we realize who we truly are. We have to learn to accept life's harsh realities, because it's going to be hard and it's going to be painful. You are going to lose a loved one. You or someone you know is going to get injured. You're going to face challenges at work and in your relationships. It has to be that way because you cannot become who you were truly intended to be without that struggle. It is in the struggle that we begin to identify who we really are and become a point of connection with other people.

If you've been asking yourself, *How do I avoid the pain?* I'm here to tell you that you can't. But if you use the pain to find your true identity, you will begin to enjoy the journey of your life in a way you never could have scripted for yourself. Because the script of your life is being written right now. The questions you have to ask yourself are: How much am I going to contribute to that script? Am I going to allow someone else or an outside influence to determine my course, or am I going to be the captain of my own ship?

I believe you can take ownership of your life if you learn to overcome ridicule, self-consciousness, and the naysayers and begin to realize you have a seed of greatness that can never be taken from you because you are created for something special. You have to learn to see yourself for the one-of-a-kind creation you are. What you have to say and contribute can't be done by anyone else but you.

When you tap into your seed of greatness, you'll be able to overcome all the relationship challenges, professional setbacks, and need for control you experience. You'll navigate your life in a way that reflects your confidence in your ability to add value to the world around you. You will live a life of meaning.

That confidence will guide you through moments of desperation and pain. You will feel it in moments when you think everything is all wrong. You will know that underneath all of the pain, you are writing a chapter of your story you will revisit when you need to be reminded of your own uniqueness, your own strength, and your own extraordinary ability to persevere.

You know what you need to do. You have seen where my twenty-year journey of finding myself has taken me. Now it's just a matter of taking the lessons I've learned and using them to empower yourself into action. Action is, after all, the greatest weapon we have in our toolbox. You can start by taking the first steps toward becoming the person you were meant to be and sharing that with the world. There's nothing stopping you from being that person. As long as you're willing to put in the time and effort, you will become who you were created to be.

There is nothing you can't overcome.

APPENDIX

The following books are my reading recommendations either for when you're doing your own 52-in-52 Challenge or when you just need a little inspiration or motivation:

1. *No Ego: How Leaders Can Cut the Cost of Workplace Drama, End Entitlement, and Drive Big Results* by Cy Wakeman
2. *The 21 Irrefutable Laws of Leadership* by John Maxwell
3. *Atomic Habits: An Easy and Proven Way to Build Good Habits and Break Bad Ones* by James Clear
4. *Can't Hurt Me: Master Your Mind and Defy the Odds* by David Goggins
5. *A Pawn's Journey: Transforming Lives One Move at a Time* by Elliott Neff
6. *Healthy Money: Making a Successful Transition from Resident to Attending* by John W. Crane
7. *Dialogue: The Art of Thinking Together* by William Isaacs
8. *Winning: The Unforgiving Race to Greatness* by Tim S. Grover
9. *Halftime: Moving from Success to Significance* by Bob Buford
10. *The Road Less Stupid: Advice from the Chairman of the Board* by Keith J. Cunningham

11. *Never Split the Difference: Negotiating as If Your Life Depended on It* by Chris Voss

12. *The Dream Manager* by Matthew Kelly

13. *Start with Why: How Great Leaders Inspire Everyone to Take Action* by Simon Sinek

14. *The 7 Habits of Highly Effective People (30th Anniversary Edition)* by Stephen R. Covey

15. *Cured: Strengthen Your Immune System and Heal Your Life* by Jeffrey Rediger

16. *The Power of Awareness: Unlocking the Law of Attraction (Deluxe Edition)* by Neville Goddard

17. *Effortless: Make It Easier to Do What Matter Most* by Greg McKeown

18. *The Obstacle is the Way: The Timeless Art of Turning Trials into Triumph* by Ryan Holiday

19. *You Are a Badass at Making Money: Master the Mindset of Wealth* by Jen Sincero

20. *The Power of Intention: Learning to Co-Create Your World Your Way* by Dr. Wayne Dyer

21. *How Successful People Think: Change Your Thinking, Change your Life* by John Maxwell

22. *Becoming Supernatural: How Common People Are Doing the Uncommon* by Dr. Joe Dispenza

23. *The Power of TED*: *The Empowerment Dynamic (10th Anniversary Edition)* by David Emerald

24. *How to Be a Great Boss* by Gino Wickman and René Boer

25. *Blue Ocean Strategy: How to Create Uncontested Market Space and Make Competition Irrelevant* by W. Chan Kim and Renée Mauborgne

26. *Blue Ocean Shift: Beyond Competing—Proven Steps to Inspire Confidence and Seize New Growth* by W. Chan Kim and Renée Mauborgne

ABOUT THE AUTHOR

Nationally renowned lawyer and entrepreneur LUIS SCOTT is the managing partner and COO of Bader Scott Injury Lawyers and CEO of 8 Figure Firm Consulting, LLC. Over this career, he's helped thousands of families in legal need. Now Scott is using his life experience to inspire others to become the people they are truly meant to be by viewing their pain as a catalyst for growth.

A native of Puerto Rico, Scott came to the United States at a young age where he went on to be recruited to play baseball for the University of West Georgia. Through his journey from the ballfield to the courtroom, he's overcome adversity including racism, naysayers, professional setbacks, and more as he discovered his true purpose and passion.

Scott is a married father of three and an avid reader who loves rooting for the Braves.

Made in the USA
Las Vegas, NV
30 April 2024

89324199R00111